For every dear reader who has written or emailed
or pulled me aside to ask,
"Where is God when it hurts?"
Your stories, your vulnerability, your tears—
and the God who has seen each one—
are the inspiration behind this book.

And
for Alena, Amanda, and Ellen—
I can't begin to understand the depths to which
you have come to know my Lord through your sufferings…
but I am privileged to be able to tell your stories
and help each of you leave a legacy
of an enduring faith in Christ.

Acknowledgments

Thank you, Shane White of Harvest House Publishers, for sharing with me your vision for a book called *When God Sees Your Tears*. Your burden and passion for this book and the women who would be touched by it have moved my heart and through the writing of this book, caused me to experience God in a greater way. My prayer is that *When God Sees Your Tears* will not only find its way into the hands of the women you had hoped, but that God will do exceedingly, abundantly beyond all you and I could ask or imagine with it—for His glory.

And thank you to my husband, Hugh, for working hard and ministering to your wife, your daughter, and countless others all these years as a pastor, teacher, counselor, listener, and friend—so I could have the freedom and flexibility to write from my heart. My ministry is *our* ministry…every step of the way.

WHEN GOD SEES YOUR TEARS

CINDI McMENAMIN

HARVEST HOUSE PUBLISHERS
EUGENE, OREGON

Cover by Dugan Design Group, Bloomington, Minnesota

Cover photo © 2010 Anna Nemoy (Xaomena) / Flickr Open / Getty Images

WHEN GOD SEES YOUR TEARS
Copyright © 2014 by Cindi McMenamin
Published by Harvest House Publishers
Eugene, Oregon 97402
www.harvesthousepublishers.com

Library of Congress Cataloging-in-Publication Data
McMenamin, Cindi, 1965-
When God sees your tears / Cindi McMenamin.
    pages cm
Includes bibliographical references.
ISBN 978-0-7369-5667-3 (pbk.)
ISBN 978-0-7369-5668-0 (eBook)
1. Christian women—Religious life. 2. Suffering—Religious aspects—Christianity. I. Title.
BV4527.M43277 2014
248.8'6—dc23
                                                                2013045582

Printed in the United States of America

14 15 16 17 18 19 20 21 22 / VP-JH / 10 9 8 7 6 5 4 3 2 1

Contents

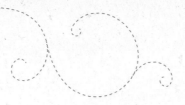

As the Tears Fall

Where is God when it hurts?

I know you've asked that question. Maybe not consciously. But in your heart of hearts, you wonder, at times, if He really cares and if He's really listening as you've cried out to Him.

Why hasn't He come through for you? Why hasn't He given you what you've begged Him for? Why do the prayers continue to be prayed and the tears continue to fall?

I too have asked those questions—when my parents divorced, as I lost the man I thought I was going to marry, as I struggled with trying to have a child, and while I endured seasons of loneliness. I know in my mind and heart that God has never left me. But there were—and are—times I'd like to get to that place where the tears no longer fall.

I have never heard God's audible voice giving me an answer to my questions through the years. But I have countless times felt His comforting presence during the long days and lonely nights, assuring me that He sees it all, He knows what's coming next, and He really *is* capable of carrying me through it.

I won't presume to know what has caused *your* tears or what is on your heart as you hold this book in your hands. But I'm guessing at the core of your heartache is a past of unresolved hurts, an unrealized dream, a crushing disappointment, or the loss of something or someone you loved. In some ways you feel it's the end of life as you know it. And yet you are not on your own, at the whim of fate or your circumstances.

In Psalm 56:8, David the songwriter, shepherd boy, and king wrote:

> You number my wanderings;
> Put my tears into Your bottle;
> Are they not in Your book? (NKJV).

Not only does God know about each tear you shed, but He *collects* them, meaning not one of them falls without His notice. Scripture also tells us God has recorded all the days of your life in His book and thinks precious thoughts of you that are too numerable to mention (Psalm 139:16-18). Jesus Himself said in Matthew 10:30 that even the very hairs on your head are numbered.

God is intimately acquainted with all the details of your life. He knows you. He hears you. He sees you. And in His infinite knowledge of you He evidently considers your tears, at the moment, more valuable to Him and your eternal good than giving to you what it is you are hoping for.

As women, it's easy for us to get lost in the drama of us and miss the real, life-changing story—the story God is weaving in our lives about Himself and what He can do when we give our tears to Him. Through the pages of this book I want to encourage you to trust Him with your story...a story that is perhaps in the conflict stage or at the crisis point. Yet God is working toward a concluding chapter that I am convinced will astonish you, even though at this point it may seem to you as if it's hardly possible. I'm convinced that when we give our stories to God from beginning to end, tears and all, He takes our longings—and our losses—and turns them into a legacy.

I want to leave a legacy in my life in spite of the tears that have fallen. And I believe that is ultimately your goal too—to live well, please God in all things, and influence others in a way that changes their world. However, in the day-to-day struggles of life, it's natural for all of us, at times, to simply desire happiness and fulfillment.

For the past 30 years, I've been helping women set meaningful goals for their lives. And frankly, many times our primary goal in life isn't deep enough. To desire marriage or marital fulfillment isn't enough. To want a baby or to raise good and respectful children, or to be remembered as a good mom or a generous woman is shallow, at best. Our goal cannot simply be to achieve a dream or reputation or what we—or the world around us—measure as success. God wants something more of your life and mine. He wants our lives to be stories that give glory and praise to Himself. As our Creator, that is His prerogative. But here's the secret—bringing glory to God with our lives brings immeasurable joy to us as well!

I want to remind you, through these pages, that the outcome or end result of what God is doing in your life through your pain isn't the only thing that's important to Him. He cares very much about what is happening in you *right now* as you're undergoing the molding process. Don't miss the wonder of what God is doing in you at this moment by looking to the someday of when it will all make sense. Treasure what you can learn in the here and now and experience joy as you travel through this process.

As we begin this journey together I want you to hold onto this comforting realization: God loves a broken heart. He doesn't love that we have to *experience* one, but He loves what happens as we are broken and moldable, completely empty, and desperate for Him. It is then that He can fill us with what He most wants us to possess—Himself!

In the pages ahead, I will share the story of one woman in the Bible whose longing for something was so intense that she offered it back to God, regardless of the cost. We will look at what prompted her to get that desperate, how she made her "deal" with God, and how God responded. We will also look at the legacy that God wove into her life through her longing and her eventual loss.

Throughout this book I will also share with you the stories of women, like you, who have cried out to God—many times in anger or confusion—when they were experiencing times of stress, difficulty, unexplainable pain, or searing loss. Some of them have seen God come through for them in remarkable ways. Some are still, by faith, waiting to see the "good" God will bring out of their situations. But all of them have experienced God's presence and power through their tears.

You will hear from women who have longed for a child and saw God do the impossible. Women who have lost their husbands and seen God take up that role in their life. Women who have been diagnosed with terminal diseases and found His joy in spite of it all. And their secret to joy can become yours too.

Through these women you are about to meet, you will be convinced that when God sees your tears (spoiler alert: He already has), there is hope. When God sees your tears, there is comfort. When God sees your tears, there is transformation. And when God sees your tears, He is just beginning the process of turning your heartache into hope and your loss into a legacy. Are you ready to discover what that legacy might be? Maybe you just need some comfort and hope to make it through today. Whatever it is your heart is longing for, I want to help. Take my hand and come with me, dear reader, on a journey that will prayerfully give you relief, hope, and tears of joy at a greater understanding of this God who loves you and desires that you ultimately become all He has designed you to be.

God *can* bring a legacy from your loss. Let me show you *how*...

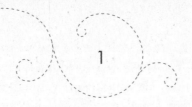

The Missing Piece

When You're Staring at the Void

To Hannah he would give a double portion,
for he loved Hannah,
but the LORD had closed her womb.

1 SAMUEL 1:5 (NASB)

I know you can feel the void. It's probably why you picked up this book. Something—or someone—is missing in your life. And it hurts.

We all sense the void, at times. For some of us it's a large, aching hole in our hearts from the absence of something we've longed for all our lives, or the loss of someone or something we don't feel we can live without. It consumes our thoughts and casts shadows over our days. For others, it's a small, festering wound that continues to remind us, now and then, that something is missing.

Lissa is a woman who never considered there might be a void in her life. Until she felt she lost everything.

Lissa felt like the luckiest girl alive as she stood at the altar on her wedding day and exchanged vows with "Jay"—the man she loved and believed she would spend the rest of her life with. Still in her mid-twenties, she was a new bride and looking forward to her happily ever after.

"Little did I know what awaited me in our first week of marriage," Lissa said.

I'll let her tell you her story in her own words:

"Over the next few days I discovered my husband was severely addicted to pain pills. He couldn't even function without them. Being newly married, I was so confused and hurt about finding this out that I didn't know what to do. I just kept telling myself *I can't lose him. I love him too much.* Besides, what would I do without him?

"So, instead of turning to God in faith that He could give me direction and wisdom on how to handle this, I turned to my own strength and tried to save my marriage on my own. I started working more than 90 hours a week to pay the bills while my husband, who was too incapacitated to work, was trying to get clean of his addiction. It was three months of nearly constant fighting and tears and never even feeling like I was married, let alone a newlywed. Once he got clean, things started to look brighter until I realized he was a completely different person when he was off of the drugs.

"He became distant and appeared uncaring. In fact, I never felt loved again. Resentment started to creep in as I began feeling used by him and like nothing more than an object to satisfy his physical and sexual needs. I worked constantly, asking for his help day after day, only to come home to a messy house, three dogs to care for, and a feeling of exhaustion and hopelessness from getting so little sleep. Jay started working at a friend's family farm (for very little pay), and after that, I barely saw him at all. I found myself pleading with him to at least be home when I got home so he could spend a little time with me in the evenings.

"Then, just four months after we married, I discovered I was pregnant. He seemed excited about the news until I mentioned that he needed to start looking for a job that was stable and paid on a regular basis. A month later, I was diagnosed with Lieden Factor 5—a blood-clotting disorder that causes complications during pregnancy. Suddenly I had a high-risk pregnancy and could no longer work more than 40 hours a week or lift more than 20 pounds. Once Jay found out I could no longer support the two of us financially, all we did was argue and all I did was cry.

"Another month went by and Jay became even more distant than ever. The more I asked for help, the more hostile he became. So he moved back home with his parents, leaving me alone with the financial responsibilities. I texted and called him every day, asking him to come home. My family tried to help, and we started marriage counseling. After Jay and I attended three sessions, I became hospitalized and couldn't pay for the counseling anymore. When I asked Jay to pay for the counseling, he refused. Shortly after, I had to move out of our house and move home with my mom because I couldn't afford to pay rent with all the medical bills I had accrued, plus the monthly living expenses that I was still trying to manage on my own.

"After pleading with Jay to work it out with me and at least try to get a job so we could be a family, he told me he didn't love me anymore and never would. He told me to stop calling and texting him. He did say he wanted to be a part of our child's life, but since that response I haven't heard from him.

"When all this started, I battled with thoughts like *Why is this happening to me? I loved him, God—why did You take him away especially now when I am pregnant? Why didn't You let it end before a baby was involved?*

"I cried a lot and felt alone and helpless. I remember just hating life. Every day that I didn't hear from Jay was increasingly more painful. I started attending church with my family, and to be honest, at that time I didn't know whether to hate God or run to Him for help. I was miserable."

What woman expects to be pregnant, abandoned, and feeling hopeless just six months after being married? Lissa was living what appeared to be a nightmare. Feeling she had no other choice, no other place to go, she finally poured out her heart to God.

"I was bitter," she said. "I didn't want to live. I lost my husband. I lost my job. I lost my house. I almost lost my dog. I nearly lost the baby. It was one defeat after another. I told my mom I just wanted my life back, and I wanted to feel normal again. My mom came alongside me and told me she knew what I was going through was hard, but I needed to bring my circumstances to God, pour out my heart to Him, and trust Him with everything that was going on."

Finding Her Way Out

Once Lissa started taking her pain to God, instead of bottling it up inside of her, she began to emerge from her slump of discouragement.

"I started pouring out my heart to God and looking to His Word for hope," she said. And she began to see God come through—and provide for her—in one situation after another.

Just a few months before her son was born, Lissa said:

"Right now, my mom, brother, and I have never been a stronger unit that wants to serve the Lord no matter how hard life may be. We are struggling to make ends meet, I have a baby who will be here soon, and we have no money to finish the room downstairs, let alone for food or gas this week, but I am at such peace knowing that God is in control that I can't even describe it. God has provided everything I need. He is still writing my story. Yes, I am scared sometimes and I still cry and feel alone, but now when I do, I praise Him for the blessings I do have. I have a house to live in, a car to drive, a job to provide income, but most of all a family and a loving God who won't ever leave me even when my mistakes and pride get in the way. He will always work things out for His good in my life."

Even though her circumstances were uncertain at that point, Lissa was putting her hope in the certainty of her God and His track record of faithfulness: "God is going to bring me out of the darkness. I don't know what is going to happen in the days ahead, but my trust is in Him alone, and that is so freeing! I praise God for bringing me back to Him, and I pray He continues to guide and teach me so I can be the mom my son needs and can look up to. I'm so afraid for when he is born, but I know he is not mine, but God's. It's hard to give that fearfulness to Him, but God has a plan and Jesus won't fail me. He will see me through. No life is more secure than a life that is surrendered to God."

Despite the stress that Lissa was experiencing, and the complications of her blood-clotting condition, a one-month hospitalization, her orders for complete bed rest, and the constant monitoring of her pregnancy beginning at 26 weeks, she was able to carry her baby for 37 weeks and give birth to a perfectly healthy but tiny 5-pound, 9-ounce son. She named him Samuel Isaiah because of how she found comfort in the Bible's story of Hannah and her child, Samuel, and because of how God's Word, in the book of Isaiah, comforted her during her pregnancy.

Even now, Lissa can see the blessings God has already bestowed on her and little Samuel. "Every time I come in for a visit, my doctor is just speechless. She said Samuel is the healthiest baby and she's never seen anything like this, in light of all the problems I had during pregnancy."

Does Lissa still cry out to God and trust that He sees her tears? Absolutely.

"I haven't heard from my husband for quite a long time. I've just been praying and trusting that God has a plan for our lives. My mom and brother and also church friends

"God is faithful, and I know He loves me."

have been so supportive that right now all I can do is thank God for everything even in the midst of wishing I had my husband at my side. God is gracious, loving, and merciful, and He knows my husband's heart. All I can do is trust."

Although Lissa's husband is absent from her life, she realizes what God has given to her in the meantime: "Right now God's answer is not a *yes* to restoring my marriage, but it is a *yes* to restoring my faith and trust in Jesus. Every time I feel defeated or start to worry about things or what is going to come of custody for my son and how I will pay for a lawyer to help, or how I will even pay for diapers, I praise God through listening to songs, quoting Scripture, and reading His Word and books of encouragement. I fill my thoughts with Him instead of the 'what ifs.' It isn't easy and I have a long way to go, but God is faithful, and I know He loves me."

Throughout her ordeal, including her abandonment, her high-risk pregnancy, and the uncertainty about her future, Lissa has claimed Isaiah 49:15-16 as God's promise to her:

> Can a mother forget the baby at her breast
>   and have no compassion on the child she has
>   borne?
> Though she may forget,
>   I will not forget you!
> See, I have engraved you on the palms of my
>   hands;
>   your walls are ever before me.

"Even though I have no idea what the years ahead may bring, I know God has a plan and purpose for me, and He will enable me to keep running the race even when I feel defeated," Lissa said.

At the time of this writing, just a year from the day she married, she holds her son (whom she calls her "little peanut") in her arms and faces life as a single mom who is confident in her son's Capable Heavenly Father—a Father who protects her, loves her, and will always come through for her and her son.

"Just last week we were out of diapers. And someone [a long-time friend of her mother's] who didn't know we were all out gave us three boxes of diapers just in time. When I asked her how she knew, she said she was praying and felt compelled to bring diapers for the new baby. One thing I've learned in the past year is to have total dependence on God and to not be too proud to receive help when it's offered. God broke me of my pride of not wanting to let others know I needed help. Since I began admitting to God that I needed His help—and the help of others—my whole walk with God has changed."

Why the Hurt Comes

Think about it. If we felt complete in every way, and our lives were simply wonderful, would we really *need* God? Of course we would. Our very existence depends on Him and without a faith and trust in Christ, we have no ability to stand righteous before a holy God, let alone get through life in a way that pleases Him and live to the potential for which He created us. But it is human nature for us to forget God—and our true need for Him—when everything in our life is lovely. And God knows that. He knows that when we're pretty comfortable—physically, emotionally, and financially—we are less likely to depend on Him for our protection, for our provision, for wisdom to make the right choices. God knows if we're not hurting in some way, frustrated in some way, *desperate* in some way, we won't cling to Him. And He knows what it will take in each of our lives for us to recognize the huge void within us...and allow Him to fill it.

As imperfect humans, we tend to think we know what will fill that void, that missing piece. For you it might be a love that you've longed for. For your friend it might be the emotional connection or harmony she is searching for in her marriage. For the woman you work with it might be a child she longs to hold in her arms. For still others it may be a dream they long to achieve, a measure of success they hope to attain, or a burning purpose they feel they have yet to discover.

We each have a different definition of what we believe is our missing piece—that one wish come true that we believe will make our lives fulfilling and complete. Yet God sees a missing piece in us that is far more extraordinary, has far more eternal consequences than the temporary fixes we seek. He sees a dependence on Him that we have yet to experience, a transformation He has been waiting to make, a legacy He wants us to leave behind when we die, a vessel of potential glory for Himself that He knows best how to use.

At 22 years old, I believed my missing piece was a husband who would make me feel complete. All around me, friends were getting engaged or married, and I had just broken up with a boyfriend of four years. I remember that ache—and fear of lifelong loneliness. Looking back now, I was ridiculously young to be so fearful that I would spend my life alone. But at the time, the ache—and fears—were intense.

I met Hugh that same summer, and we were engaged and married within a year of meeting each other. At that point I had a career job, a husband, and a promise of a happily ever after, so I figured I had all I needed to be content for the rest of my days. But four years into my marriage (to a pastor, nonetheless!), I realized a man cannot fill the deep recesses of my soul in the way God was meant to. I had to find that my fulfillment and sense of completion can only come from Him.[1] And when we give the Lord first place in our lives, He has a way of filling us with joy and strength—just as He had done for Lissa.

Within each of us is a void that cries out for fulfillment. You are not the only one experiencing that—a void from unmet expectations, or a failed marriage, or the death of a child, or the loss of a dream, or the desire for that "something more." It's that part of our life that we feel will be complete *if only*... And God is the only One who can fill that void with whatever it is we are asking for. But sometimes, in order to get us to seek Him, He decides not to. Such was the case with Hannah.

Hannah's Missing Piece

Hannah felt a void in her life too. Her story is recorded in the Bible in the beginning chapters of 1 Samuel and touches our hearts because of how desperately she cried out to God for what she wanted. She pleaded with Him to fill an intense void and give her a child. All around her, women were giving birth to babies and raising children.

But Hannah couldn't conceive a child. In case you're not familiar with her story, let me give you some background.

Hannah had a husband, Elkanah, who loved her. Scripture implies he loved her even more than his other wife, Peninnah. I know, that's strange, but they lived in a part of the world where polygamy was culturally acceptable. It certainly wasn't God's design for His people, but it was permitted by Jewish law under certain circumstances, which might explain why Elkanah had two wives.[2] But even though Hannah was loved by her husband, she longed for something more. She wanted to have a child. And she lived in a culture that considered it a shame and reproach for a woman to be childless. To make matters worse, her husband's other wife, Peninnah, had children and would provoke Hannah to tears because she was without a child.

Follow the story with me:

> When the day came that Elkanah sacrificed, he would give portions to Peninnah his wife and to all her sons and her daughters; but to Hannah he would give a double portion, for he loved Hannah, *but the* Lord *had closed her womb*. Her rival, however, would provoke her bitterly to irritate her, *because the* Lord *had closed her womb*. It happened year after year, as often as she went up to the house of the Lord, she would provoke her; so she wept and would not eat (1 Samuel 1:4-7 nasb).

Hannah's husband tried to console her by saying, in a sense, "Why are you so upset? You have *me*. What more could you want?" (I *know* what you're thinking at this point. But hold that thought…we'll get to Hannah's husband in chapter 3.) The story goes on to say that Hannah pulled herself together, ate and drank, and then found a quiet place to pour out her heart to God in prayer.

> And she made a vow, saying, "Lord Almighty, if you will only look on your servant's misery and remember me,

and not forget your servant but give her a son, then I will give him to the LORD for all the days of his life" (verse 11).

Hannah was not only asking God for what she believed would make her life complete, but for what would ease her suffering and torment. She was asking to be remembered, relieved, and restored. Her prayer was, in essence, "Give me this one desire of mine, and I'll give it back to You for Your glory."

We are going to come back to Hannah's story throughout this book and see how God lovingly—and surprisingly—granted her request. We will look at Hannah's heartfelt "deal" with God, how she handled a misunderstanding as she was making that deal, and the risks she took—years later—by following through with her vow to God. We will also look at what God was divinely orchestrating with an entire nation of people that may have prompted God to withhold a baby from Hannah long enough for her to get desperate enough to make that deal with God. But for now, let's look at a pivotal phrase in that story that may help you understand what God might be doing in *your* life as He sees your tears.

Four Disturbing Words

There were some disturbing words in the Bible passage we looked at a moment ago. Did you notice them? There were seven words in that narrative that cut me to the core: "because the Lord had closed her womb."

Four of those seven words cut *all* of us to the core in one way or another as they become a narrative of *our* lives as well: "*because the Lord had…*"

Dear reader, I would feel so much better if that sentence about Hannah read "because she was unable to bear children." But that verse specifically tells us that *the Lord* was the One withholding from Hannah the one thing she wanted so badly. God was behind the coveted missing piece in her life. He was the One who not only allowed, but *engineered* the void she was experiencing.

Now before you throw this book against the wall, thinking *That's it…I knew it. God IS the One who is responsible for my pain*—please stay with me and let me explain.

We would like to think that God is the One behind only the blessings and rewards in life and that when we stumble upon difficult times or have something withheld from us it's because of the natural consequences of a bad decision, or the unfortunate consequences of living in a fallen world, or maybe even God's *punishment* for some sin in our lives. But we have a hard time wrapping our minds around the possibility that God would allow—or even arrange—certain difficulties to come our way. Yet that is one of the primary ways He awakens our need for Him, grows our dependence on Him, shapes our character, and draws us closer to Himself.

Scripture tells us that God can do "all things, and that no purpose of [His] can be thwarted" (Job 42:2). It also tells us that "every good and perfect gift is from above, coming down from the Father of the heavenly lights, who does not change like shifting shadows" (James 1:17). So if every gift is from God, and you're praying for a "gift" and it's not arriving, God is the One who, for some reason, is deciding to withhold that gift. And I have learned through the years that some of God's "gifts" to us are the very things He decides to withhold. These "gifts" sometimes take the form of difficulties, losses, frustrations, and outright pain. Initially we don't see them as gifts, but more like disappointments, aggravations, or even rejection. But they are gifts, nonetheless, that are given to us to grow us to a new level in our spiritual life or to prepare us for something better that God has in store for us, or perhaps to even help us see something extraordinary about God that we couldn't see before.

When God's "Gift" Is *No*

I remember not wanting to accept one of the "gifts" God was giving me, primarily because I saw it as His withholding, not as His giving. I struggled with not being able to have a second child (what doctors now refer to as secondary infertility). It was a struggle for me because I remember "claiming" a verse as my promise that I would have another child: "No good thing will he withhold from those who walk uprightly" (Psalm 84:11 NASB).

I first highlighted that verse in my Bible when I prayed to the Lord and asked for Hugh to become my husband. "Lord, Hugh is a good thing, and I am walking uprightly. Certainly You will not withhold him from me." And God didn't. A year after saying that prayer, Hugh and I were married, and I can confirm that over the past 25 years Hugh has been a "good thing" in my life.

So I figured the same prayer would work when it came to having a second child. "Surely another baby is a good thing, God," I prayed. "Certainly You will not withhold that." And yet He did. Hugh and I were not able to have a second child, and in the years since, God has graciously shown me that having only one child was, and still is, His idea of "good" for me. Apparently what God considered a "good thing" was not birthing a second child, but birthing a writing and speaking ministry instead. Although at the time I felt that God was withholding something from me, today I can see His withholding as a "gift" in terms of a different life direction that He had planned for me.

Through the years I've seen, over and over again, that God's idea of a good thing (and ultimately what's best for me in my faith walk with Him) may be completely different than mine. Although my opinion has often differed from God's in His early stages of withholding something from me (for example, I know quite a few women who have both a ministry to women *and* a second or third or fifth child too!), I have learned to not question the wisdom and actions of an all-knowing, all-loving God who is much more capable of managing my life than I am.

I do not have a second child today *because the Lord has closed my womb.* But I can also say, "I am living the dream God has placed on my heart—through my writing and speaking—because the Lord has closed my womb."

I could give you a lengthy list of other "gifts" that I have received at God's hand but didn't originally see as gifts because they all included the phrase *because the Lord had…*

I didn't marry Mike *because the Lord had changed his heart.*

I lost a good friend *because the Lord had taken her away.*

I went through a season of loss *because the Lord had shut the door.*

But there are other ways of looking at those same "gifts" (or withholdings):

I married Hugh *because the Lord had changed Mike's heart.*

I was spared further hurt *because the Lord had taken her away.*

I can minister to women today *because the Lord had shut that door.*

What are some *because the Lord had* phrases that have affected your life and caused your tears to flow? Are you a woman who is where she is today…

because the Lord had closed that door?

because the Lord had changed his heart?

because the Lord had taken her away?

because the Lord didn't let you marry?

because the Lord has not healed you?

because the Lord let you get cancer?

because the Lord had not stopped it?

My friend, God has His reason for why He has allowed or prevented something from happening in your life. And it's not because He doesn't love you or care about you or hear your prayers. It's very possible that He wants to bless you from another angle. And it's very possible He wants you to realize that the one thing you need the most—your one missing piece—is Himself.

Lissa's Missing Piece

Lissa, who is now raising her child on her own and depending on God every step of the way, realizes what her missing piece was all along.

"At first I thought my missing piece was my husband. I thought my life was over and I could never find love again or even be happy again. I begged God to bring him back, and I just didn't understand why this was happening to me. But once I realized how silly and self-ish those words sounded (because I was focused on me), I discovered that the true missing piece in my life was the One I had pushed away for the past two years of my life.

"I had a mom who instilled the truth in me and always taught me that only Jesus can meet and satisfy my needs and wants and desires. But I was too prideful to listen, and I ended up letting things and the wrong people influence me. I now realize how my life had taken a downward spiral. I came to regret the decisions I had made and how I had become reliant on myself because I thought I had a good job and because I was married to a man I thought loved me, and because I was going to have a family. God had to strip me of all of that to bring me back to where I once was—to a place of total surrender to Jesus."

If you had asked Lissa a year ago why her life had taken the course it had, she might have told you, in anger or confusion, "Because the Lord let my husband leave."

And, having heard her story, you might agree that those seven words had surely changed the course of her life.

But today Lissa looks not at what God has withheld, but at the blessings He has brought to her *through* her loss. And the seven words to describe how the course of her life has changed sound differently today: "Because the Lord has shown me mercy."

I wonder if she could even say "Because the Lord has become my Husband."

Lissa says, "I still love my husband and I miss him even after all the wrong he has done. But I often wonder where I would be right now if he had worked it out with me. I know I would not have turned to my Savior, the Lord Jesus, whom I cried out to in my desperation. And all the pain and hurt I felt and am still feeling was worth it because I will be able to pass on to my son a faith that I wouldn't have if I was still with my husband."

Did you catch that?

Lissa is aware that a legacy is coming out of the loss she experienced. Through her ordeal, she came to know God intimately, and she now has a living faith and trust in the Lord that she can pass on to her son.

"God has given me a healthy baby boy, a wonderful blessing," Lissa said. "And He definitely has a plan for my little peanut. I tell my son every day he's going to grow up to be a strong, courageous man of God."

She is also resting in the fact that God is in complete control of her life's circumstances.

"God opened my womb for a reason. And there's also a reason my husband is not here, and I don't know what that is. I struggle with that, but I have to keep it in the forefront of my mind that God's in control of all of this and He knows what He's doing."

Searching for a Reason

It's in our human nature to try to figure out the reason or purpose behind our suffering. Sometimes we find ourselves saying, "If someone somewhere can gain something from what I've been through, then it will all be worthwhile." But rest assured, my friend, of these two things:

> Can you hold onto God for the beautiful result of what He is doing in and through *you*?

1. *Sometimes you won't be able to see it.* Even if you can't figure out *how* God can use whatever you are going through, that doesn't mean He can't. God may choose to give you a glimpse of what He is doing and how He is working. If He does, then thank Him for that. He has been gracious in giving you a small picture of His big plan. But God doesn't always give us a clue as to how He is working and the way He will receive glory from our lives. He is not obligated to let us know *how* He is working or *why* He is doing something. He doesn't need our

approval or our suggestions either. That is where our trust comes in. If you are surrendered to Him, He will do whatever He desires with your situation—in His own timing, and in His own way.

2. *Sometimes* you *are the one who stands to gain from what you are going through.* We tend to think that God's plan always involves "some future good" or some eternal outcome somewhere for someone else. At times we hold onto the idea of a great end result eventually pacifying our pain or bringing purpose to our suffering. And yet God is very much concerned about what is happening in you *right now* as you sort through the complexities of life and sift through your sorrow. Of course He can use your pain for good in someone else's life or for some benefit that is still future. He is God. He can do *anything.* But His process of transformation in you is just as important to Him as any end result or greater good that you are hoping to see. Can you trust the process? Can you hold onto God for the beautiful result of what He is doing in and through *you?* Can you be satisfied with *His* contentment over yours when it comes to what He is doing in your life?

Unmet Expectations

No young woman—like Lissa—imagines that she will end up becoming a struggling single mom just a year into her marriage. No little girl—like some I've met—expects to find herself without a daddy or wondering if she is really loved. No woman past her forties expects to live out the rest of her days without a husband or children or grandchildren. No one, for that matter, imagines in advance the heartaches and heartbreaks that will come their way. And yet consider the world we live in. Imperfect people. Hearts that devise wicked schemes. Selfishness. Broken promises. And in the midst of all of that is One who is still absolutely and inarguably in control.

As Lissa told me her story, her emphasis was not on the void that her husband had left, but the void that was being filled by the true

"Husband" in her life, the Lord her Maker, who has proven Himself to be her spiritual Husband, Provider, Protector and Friend.[3]

Lissa wisely came to recognize what she needed most—a dependence upon God that she never even realized she could have. And today, she is beginning to see how God has taken a huge loss in her life and is turning it into a legacy.

What About You?

I won't presume to know what your void looks like. But God knows exactly what it is…and perhaps He knows it's the only thing that is going to cause you to depend fully on Him.

One morning, as I was praying for God to fill that one void in my life that keeps surfacing as a result of unmet expectations, I remember thinking that it wasn't a huge request of God. He could easily handle it. He could grant it at any time.

And yet I will never forget the whisper I heard on my heart that morning: "My child, why would I give you the one thing that would keep you from clinging so tightly to Me?"

In the moment that I "heard" that, I wasn't disappointed that God was again saying *no*. I was, instead, overcome by His love and jealousy of me. My "unmet desire" really *is* what keeps me on my knees before Him, keeps me clinging to Him, keeps me coming up alongside His heart. And so He continues to withhold that one thing because He knows what is best for me from an eternal standpoint. He wants to remain first in my heart. He wants me to look to *Him* for what I need most. He wants to *be* the One I desire. And He is—

because the Lord has continued to withhold.

Sometimes I wonder if God withholds whatever it is that will eventually become an idol in our lives—whatever it is that might keep us from putting Him first. If God gives you a husband, will you still keep the Lord first in your life? If He gives you a child, will it take His place as first in your heart? If He allows you to live your dream, will you leave Him in the dust and live for yourself? If He eases your financial worries, will you still depend on Him for your daily bread? God knows what each of us needs—and what we should be without—in order to keep us clinging to Him. He knows—and He will allow or withhold—whatever will keep us right where we need to be when it comes to our relationship with Him.

In Hannah's case, God granted her a child. But as we will see in the coming chapters, she didn't take God's gift and wander off. She handed that same child back to God and continued to live in dependence on Him. She continued to be a woman of prayer. In fact, the granting of her request may have made her even *more* dependent on God. Is that the case with whatever you are asking God for? Will the fulfillment of your desire make you even *more* dependent on the Lord?

Wherever you are in your experience of staring at the void, I hope you will see not the disappointment or disaster in front of you, but the dependence on God that you can cultivate. That dependence on God will eventually fill any void that cries out for more. Trust Him with your tears, my friend. And trust Him with the void. Oh, how He wants to fill it with Himself!

Letting God Fill the Void

Take some time to reflect on these questions as a way of processing what you've just read and applying it to your situation.

1. In a sentence or two, try to describe what the void looks like in your life.

2. Through your void or loss, how might God want to be developing you into a person who is more dependent on Him?

3. As you consider the following ways that God wants to fill the void in your life, read the verses listed under each one (you may even want to write them out as a reminder of how God wants to fill the void in your life):

- He wants to be your emotional provider and Spiritual Husband

   Isaiah 54:5—

- He wants to be your material provider

   Philippians 4:19—

- He wants to be your heart's delight

  Psalm 37:4—

  Matthew 22:37—

- He wants to make you more like His Son

  Romans 8:28-29—

A Prayer of Invitation

If you've never surrendered your life to Jesus Christ and asked Him to fill that void in your heart, you can do that now (and if you already have, you can adapt this prayer so it speaks of rededication or recommitment):

Lord,

I know You have a plan and a purpose for my life. And I want to bring my life in alignment with Your plan and purpose. But I can't do that as long as I am holding the reins of my life. So I surrender my heart, my will, my life to You. I realize that I am a sinner, by nature, and that nothing I do can ever earn me the favor of God. It is only through Your perfect, sinless, righteous Son, Jesus Christ, and His death and resurrection for me, that I can be accepted by You. So I ask that Jesus' atoning death on the cross apply to *my* sin. Be the Lord of my life and the keeper of my heart. Help me to live from this day forward in obedience to You out of love and appreciation to You for Your tremendous sacrifice for me—allowing, and *planning in advance*, that Your Own Son die to pay the penalty for my sin and to purchase a place in heaven for me. Fill that void in my life with Yourself and become the One thing I desire so that You can trust me with the desires of my heart.

Thank You for knowing me, hearing me, and wanting me to cling to You no matter what is going on in my life. Hold me close and show me what it means to find my fulfillment in You.

The Provocation
When Your Heart Is Harassed

Her rival, however, would provoke her bitterly to irritate her,
because the LORD had closed her womb.

1 SAMUEL 1:6 (NASB)

Alena knows what it's like to be harassed. Not by another person
wanting to gloat over her. Not by an addiction that has taken her
into bondage. But by a ravaging disease we all know and fear: *cancer.*
It first hunted down her husband in the prime of his life.

Alena and her college sweetheart, Rick, married when they were
both just 20 years old. He had a passion for God and a heart for
ministry and became a pastor. He was in his second church, struggling to make ends meet, when he took on a second job to help
them out financially. Alena was pregnant with their second child
when Rick began taking a series of tests to determine why he wasn't
recovering from what he thought was a sinus infection. After several
months and multiple tests, Rick was diagnosed with colon and liver
disease and was told he had only two-and-a-half years to live. Alena
remembers the long, silent drive home from the hospital, where her
husband had remained because of his condition.

"That night, two hours away from my husband, I lay in bed with
my newborn son and my three-year-old cradled against me and
cried out to God. I wanted God to spare my husband's life so he
could see our boys grow up and so we could grow old together. We

were both twenty-five years old and had our whole lives ahead of us. It didn't seem fair. No. It *wasn't* fair. I cried myself to sleep as the night swallowed me up."

Sometime later, God directed Alena's attention to Joshua 1:9: "Have I not commanded you? Be strong and courageous. Do not be afraid; do not be discouraged, for the LORD your God will be with you wherever you go."

"I didn't understand at the time why I was directed to that Scripture passage," Alena said. "But I knew that God was encouraging me to stay strong and trust Him. He was with us no matter what happened. I clung to those words for a very, very long time."

Rick did not die in two-and-a-half years as the doctors predicted. He held on for another ten, living life to the fullest amidst constant health complications. Throughout those years, Rick went back to Bible college and finished his degree, served as a pastor in various churches, and had two more children with Alena.

"There were numerous hospital stays and scares. We barely got by financially, and yet we were happy," Alena said. "We trusted God completely, and He supplied all of our needs."

Rick and Alena moved to Pennsylvania, where they lived for five years as Rick took an associate pastor and worship/youth leader position, thinking it might be less stressful than being a full-time senior pastor. But he was just as busy as ever, and on the move constantly.

"In all of it, Rick was vivacious and lived life as if each day were his last," Alena said. "He was so upbeat that most people who met him didn't know he was so ill. Despite the fourth party in our marriage, called *disease*, we were very happy and joyful. And through it all, he was an amazing husband and father."

But on New Year's Eve in 1999, Alena felt that God was beginning to prepare her for what was to come.

"We stood on our porch watching people set off small fireworks. Our kids were running around the yard, excited to be up late. As we stood there watching them play, Rick asked what I saw for us as a family in 2000. I told him I wasn't sure, but deep inside I felt like we were going to experience a big change. He wanted to know what kind. Was it going to be a move? Or something else? I didn't know, but whatever it was, I felt like it was going to be life-changing."

Their life-change happened early in the fall. Rick woke up one September morning not feeling well, and his stomach was extremely distended.

"We both knew something was not right, but figured it was another bout of his disease flaring up," Alena said. They called his specialist and were told to come in immediately so Rick could have tests taken and blood work done.

"On October 3, 2000, we sat in the doctor's office, and the medical staff were quite concerned. When they sent Rick to the lab for blood work, the doctor pulled me aside. He asked if I was strong, and I said that I thought so. With great sternness, he told me I needed to be extremely strong because Rick had lymphoma. It wouldn't be long before his life was over. All I could manage to say was 'What about our kids?'

"This was *not* supposed to happen," Alena said. "With all of Rick's health issues, he was strong, even physically, and doing well, considering his condition. We, including his specialist, were all devastated. They set up an appointment with the cancer center and sent us home. Walking hand in hand, we left in silence and in a fog of emotions on that sunny October day. It was strange to see things look so normal outside when inside of us nothing would ever be normal again. We were facing an unknown future—again."

Rick was admitted to the cancer center in Pittsburgh on October 22, 2000. When doctors asked him what he wanted out of his

"I told him that the kids and I would be fine because God would take good care of us."

treatment, he told them he had a family who needed him, "so give me all you've got."

Rick went through several rounds of chemotherapy, but it became apparent within a week or two that he wasn't going to survive.

"I knew, deep in my soul, that this was it," Alena said. "But I continued to cry out to God. I told God I didn't want Rick to die. We needed him. The kids needed him. As the days went by, I saw the suffering, and I didn't want him to suffer. I surrendered him to God, telling the Lord if He wanted Rick, He could have him. That was the hardest prayer I had ever prayed."

Rick passed away on Thanksgiving Day that same year—just 33 days after his diagnosis of lymphoma. When Alena arrived at the hospital that afternoon, she was told that he had been waiting for her.

"I walked in not knowing what to expect. He was still unconscious. I went to his side and told him how much I loved him and it was okay if he wanted to see Jesus. I told him that the kids and I would be fine because God would take good care of us. I also told him to go home [to heaven] and I would catch up to him later. No sooner did I speak those words than he took his last breath.

"At the age of thirty-seven, I was now alone and a single mother of four kids, ages eight through fifteen. All I knew was that God was going to have to help me and give me strength. I had to be strong and courageous and know that He would be with me."

A few years later, Alena remarried. Rick made her promise to him, when he was first diagnosed with lymphoma, that she would open her heart and remarry someone who would take care of her and the children. I would like to tell you that Alena then entered her happily ever after with beautiful memories of her first husband, Rick, and a future full of life, love, and happiness with her second husband, Peter. But on the twelfth anniversary of Rick's diagnosis with lymphoma, Alena sat in the doctor's office with Peter, and this time the provocation was even more personal. Cancer had reared its ugly head again—this time on *her*.

Alena was told she had a tumor in her brain. And during her diagnosis, all she remembered was feeling blanketed in peace. Instead of feeling as though she were losing her footing, she said, "The ground felt even more solid beneath me. It was God who was leading me through it."

"Twelve years prior, Rick and I sat in the doctor's office as they told us he had lymphoma. Who knew that twelve years later to the day, on October 3, my husband, Peter, and I would be sitting hand-in-hand in the neurologist's office as he confirmed that I had a brain tumor?"

As the doctor talked with Alena about her tumor, Alena remembers hearing another "voice" deep inside of her. "It was as if there were two distinct conversations going on at the same time—my doctor's diagnosis and the Lord's voice, through Scripture, on my heart:

> "For my thoughts are not your thoughts,
>   neither are your ways my ways,"
>   declares the LORD.
> "As the heavens are higher than the earth,
>   so are my ways higher than your ways
>   and my thoughts than your thoughts"
>   (Isaiah 55:8-9).

"A deep sense of peace and resolution came over me," Alena said. "Was I scared? *You bet.* Did my trust in God outweigh my fear? Yes, it did. I had already lived through enough heartache to know that God is bigger than anything I face and fear. If this was the journey I was to take, I knew with confidence He would be with me."

Unexplainable Joy

As Alena underwent chemotherapy—in spite of her fear because of how quickly her husband had died after his chemo started—she continued to keep her focus on the One who was in control of her body, health, and life.

"I have days when I'm sad, but I can't help but talk about the Lord and the joy He has given me during the storm," she said. "There are days when the waves are crashing and it feels like the ship is sinking, but there is still joy."

Negative thoughts will play in Alena's head at times, saying, *You're washed up. You're used up. You're not needed. What can God do with you now? Look at you. Your brain tumor has restricted you and everything you had plans to do.*

But Alena chooses to focus on the truth rather than the lies. And the truth is that God *is* using her to encourage and inspire others and to minister to people in an even greater capacity than ever before. She is repeatedly told that she is an inspiration to others because of her constant joy in spite of what she's been through. She remembers being told that years ago as well when Rick was battling his health problems.

"I guess people think I *should* be downcast," Alena said. "I will use Scripture God has placed on my heart and speak of His greatness. I have met people on the Internet, and through Facebook, and on brain tumor sites, and have shared my story with them. There are a lot of people who are downcast because they don't have hope. They don't know God. I'm able to share my hope with them."

Alena still has days when she brings her tears before the Lord.

"God didn't say *yes* to my complete healing. Am I disappointed? Very much so. Impatient? Yes, because I wanted to move on with life. Scared? Yes. Anxious? Of course. Did I want to run from it? You bet!" And yet she continues to seek instruction from God's Word on how to persevere.

"At times, I am bummed," she said. "I would like to get off this hamster wheel I feel like I'm on. But recently I was reminded of Philippians 4:8: 'Finally, brothers and sisters, whatever is true, whatever is noble, whatever is right, whatever is pure, whatever is lovely, whatever is admirable—if *anything is excellent or praiseworthy—think about such things.*'

"That was my aha moment," she said. "I have plenty of things in my life that are worthy of praise. So I'm thinking on *those* things and asking God to cover what is going on now. I have plenty of reasons to trust Him."

These days, Alena often emails me and shares with me her "God moments" and how the Lord is continuing to shape her, through all that she has experienced, into the image of Christ:

"God has been so gracious and kind, and He has been my undeniable strength for an unexpected journey," she told me recently. "I do feel so much more aware of the Holy Spirit moving in my life…there is a sense of expectancy…I can't quite explain it. I'm trying to listen and act."

This morning, as I write her story in this book, it's October 3— the one-year anniversary of her brain tumor diagnosis and the thirteenth anniversary of her husband's diagnosis of lymphoma. Today her email to me, and her status on Facebook, read:

> How do I look at this day? By all accounts, I should hate this day. In reality, it's a day marked by bad news. The truth? I do not look at it with fear, hate, nor dread, but with a joyous heart. I trust in an unfailing God for today and all the days to come. He continues to be my joy and strength. Psalm 32:10: "The LORD's unfailing love surrounds the one who trusts in him." Jeremiah 29:11: "'I know the plans I have for you,' declares the LORD, 'plans to prosper you and not to harm you, plans to give you hope and a future.'" He never left me then and He won't leave me now. He says, "Never will I leave you nor forsake you" (Hebrews 13:5).

Where Is *Your* Trust?

Do you remember what I suggested in chapter 1? God knows that when everything is going well in our lives we tend to think we don't need Him. Here is a woman who has been hurt through cancer's ravaging effects on her first husband's body and now on hers, yet she is quieting herself against Him, clinging to His Word and His promises, and trusting Him with her very life.

You and I may not have been diagnosed with a tumor...yet. But like Alena, we must be trusting the Lord with *our* very lives. Because healthy or not, God wants complete surrender from each of us. And He will, at times, allow us to be provoked to the point of surrender if that's what it takes for us to be more closely knit together with Him.

Hannah's Harassment

God wanted complete surrender in Hannah's life too. She had already experienced the ache of not being able to have a child. But to make matters worse, she lived with a woman who had several children and constantly made Hannah feel inferior for not having any. Any woman who has ever longed for a child and has been inundated with pregnancy announcements and baby showers from friend after friend and family members all around her can relate to Hannah's festering wound.

Scripture tells us that every year when Elkanah took his wives to Shiloh to worship the Lord, that Peninnah—whom Scripture aptly refers to as Hannah's "rival"—saw that as her golden opportunity to really rub it in that Hannah was childless. We are told that Hannah was provoked to the point of weeping and not eating. And finally, she poured it all out in prayer to God. "In bitterness of soul" she "prayed to the Lord and wept in anguish" (1 Samuel 1:10 NKJV). Such provocation in her life led her to desperate prayer...a prayer that God heard.

We find a couple of disturbing things happening in this story, and they involve Hannah's reaction to the situation. I wonder if you and I, at times, react similarly when someone or something is provoking us!

First, Hannah *let* Peninnah provoke her. Scripture clearly tells us Peninnah's intention: "her rival kept provoking her *in order to irritate her*" (verse 6). And Peninnah was successful in her attempts, wasn't she? Is it possible that Hannah wouldn't have *continued* to be provoked this way if she hadn't let Peninnah's rude comments bother her? What if she had simply ignored Peninnah? What if she had told Peninnah, "I'm sorry your life as a mom is not as fulfilling as you want me to think it is, because you wouldn't be working so hard to make mine miserable if you were truly happy. People who are hurt themselves will hurt others. I will pray for your heart *and* your happiness"?

Instead, it appears that Hannah took Peninnah's cruel provocations to heart because Scripture says "This went on *year after year*." Her rival provoked her "till she wept and would not eat" (verse 7). Wow. Peninnah, through her pestering, gained control over Hannah's actions. She got exactly what she wanted from her. But she never would've had that control over Hannah if Hannah had not given it to her. Peninnah clearly exercised this power *every year*—to the point that Hannah would become so miserable she refused to eat.

Lessons from Hannah

We learn from Hannah's situation three lessons that will help us when we are provoked or harassed:

1. We decide how much we will let something hurt us.

Whose words are speaking the loudest to you? Your own doubts or fears, the critical words of another, the lies of the enemy? Or are you listening to the voice of truth? If Hannah had countered Peninnah's criticism or bragging by responding with the words of her husband ("Isn't my love for you better than ten sons?"), then she might have been better able to withstand Peninnah's cruelty. You and I today have much more defense than Hannah had. We have the living Word of God and one promise after another to keep us grounded in His truth and to keep us confident when we are under attack. The next time someone tries to hurt you, remember *your* heavenly Husband's words:

- "'No weapon forged against you will prevail, and you will refute every tongue that accuses you. This is the heritage of the servants of the LORD, and this is their vindication from me,' declares the LORD" (Isaiah 54:17).

- "'For I know the plans I have for you,' declares the LORD, 'plans to prosper you and not to harm you, plans to give you hope and a future'" (Jeremiah 29:11).

- "If God is for us, who can be against us?" (Romans 8:31).

2. We determine who is in control by how we respond.

Only you and I can give another person or situation the power to control our emotions, attitudes, and actions. And when we respond in anger, defensiveness, or despair (by not eating or not leaving our house, or not showing up again), we are proving to someone that they have won in their attempt to control how we feel. Hannah could've maintained control of the situation by brushing off Peninnah's behavior or praying for her. But sadly, she ended up letting her rival control her response. The next time someone tries to wield control over your emotions, remember these words and by doing so, remember who is *really* in control:

- "The Lord is my light and my salvation—whom shall I fear? The LORD is the stronghold of my life—of whom shall I be afraid?" (Psalm 27:1-2).

- "When you pass through the waters, I will be with you; and when you pass through the rivers, they will not sweep over you. When you walk through the fire, you will not be burned; the flames will not set you ablaze" (Isaiah 43:2).

- "'In your anger do not sin': Do not let the sun go down while you are still angry, and do not give the devil a foothold" (Ephesians 4:26-27).

- "Do not let any unwholesome talk come out of your mouths, but only what is helpful for building others up according to their needs, that it may benefit those who listen" (Ephesians 4:29).

- "Walk by the Spirit, and you will not gratify the desires of the flesh" (Galatians 5:16).

3. We can, at any time, bring our problems to the One who will make things right.

When we take our problems to God, instead of taking them into our own hands, we are affirming to ourselves and others the fact that He can handle them so much better than we can. When Hannah *finally* took her situation to God in prayer, that's when change happened. God didn't give her a son at that moment, but Hannah experienced the peace that comes when we release our burdens to God—burdens that we were not intended to carry. Whatever it is in your life that is harassing you—a person, an illness, a fear, a threatening situation—you are powerless to control it anyway. You might as well give it to the only One who can execute justice, and execute it swiftly. How much emotional stress would we rid ourselves of, and how much pain could we avoid, if we would just bring our problems to God? Here is your confidence in laying your burden at His feet:

- "Be anxious for nothing, but in everything by prayer and supplication with thanksgiving let your requests be made known to God. And the peace of God, which surpasses all comprehension, will guard your hearts and your minds in Christ Jesus" (Philippians 4:6-7 NASB).

- "This is the confidence we have in approaching God:

that if we ask anything according to his will, he hears us. And if we know that he hears us—whatever we ask—we know that we have what we asked of him" (1 John 5:14-15).

What Harasses *You*?

Who or what is provoking you, my friend? What is threatening your peace? A fearful diagnosis? A person who seems to have it out for you? Another woman who threatens your marriage? A critical boss who threatens your husband's well-being? Is it a job that is competing for your husband's affections or a child's struggle with drugs? Maybe it's a fear of what might be that harasses you, threatening to steal your joy and ruin your life?

As strong and fearful as cancer appears to be, Alena knows her God is stronger. She knows nothing can touch her that hasn't first passed through God's loving hands. She knows His presence is much more powerful than the threat of darkness.

We live in a world in which evil appears to be so very strong. Tears, at times, seem more real than God's comforting presence, and fear can feel larger than the power of God. I constantly hear Christians say, "Things are getting so much worse" (and you hear it too, I'm sure). But no matter how messed up this world becomes, Scripture gives us the assurance Christ is in control. Jesus Himself said, "All authority in heaven and on earth has been given to me" (Matthew 28:18). But we forget that Christ has overcome the work of the devil, that death has lost its sting (1 Corinthians 15:54-57), that there is coming a day when the Lord will make all things new (Revelation 21:5). We forget because pain and evil and sin still occur in this world and it feels, at times, as if everything is out of control.

When Darkness Appears Strong

Last weekend I heard a woman complaining about the attacks of the enemy and how he "comes in like a flood" to wreak havoc in our lives. She was referring to Satan, whom Scripture says "prowls around like a roaring lion looking for someone to devour" (1 Peter 5:8). I'm fairly certain that her words were prompted by a verse—or a song that resulted from a translation of a verse—implying that Satan, our enemy, is a fierce, powerful flood.

In Isaiah 59:19, in the King James Version, we are told: "So shall they fear the name of the Lord from the west, and his glory from the rising of the sun. *When the enemy shall come in like a flood*, the Spirit of the Lord shall lift up a standard against him."

Because of this particular translation of that verse, we sing a song in our churches about the "power of darkness" coming in like a flood. No wonder we think of Satan as a fierce, determined, intense power who is capable of ruining us.

Yet Isaiah 59:19 is actually telling us the opposite—that the power of *the Lord* is what our enemy should fear reckoning with. The verse speaks of the Lord as the One whose name is to be feared, and *He is the One who comes in like a flood and rushing wind.*

Consider that verse in the following translations, none of which mentions "the enemy," but only the Lord:

> So they will fear the name of the Lord from the west
> And His glory from the rising of the sun,
> *For He will come like a rushing stream*
> *Which the wind of the Lord drives*
> > (Isaiah 59:19 NASB).

> From the west, people will fear the name of
> > the Lord,
> > and from the rising of the sun, they will revere
> > > his glory.
> *For he will come like a pent-up flood*
> > *that the breath of the Lord drives along* (NIV).

> *He will come like a rushing stream,*
> *which the wind of the Lord drives* (ESV).

He will come like a raging flood tide
driven by the breath of the LORD (NLT).

He will attack like a flood
in a mighty windstorm
Nations in the west and the east
will then honor and praise
his wonderful name (CEV).

In the west they'll fear the name of GOD,
   in the east they'll fear the glory of GOD,
For he'll arrive like a river in flood stage,
   whipped to a torrent by the wind of GOD (MSG).

In fact, the King James and New King James versions are the only translations that use the word "enemy" in that passage, and in the New King James, a footnote declares that "when the enemy comes" could also mean "when He comes as an enemy"[1]—implying Christ's vindication and fierceness to protect His own.

The Strength of the Lord

My, how we can tend to concentrate on how "the enemy" comes in—like a powerful, overwhelming flood. And yet Scripture places the emphasis on the power of the Lord, which sometimes "comes as an enemy."

Furthermore, Isaiah 54:17 tells us:

No weapon that is formed against you will prosper;
And every tongue that accuses you in judgment you
   will condemn.
This is the heritage of the servants of the LORD,
And their vindication is from Me (NASB).

And in the New Testament we are told, "If God is for us, who can be against us?" (Romans 8:31).

Have you also heard other followers of Christ give more credit to

Satan than he deserves? Think about how many times you've heard someone say:

- "We've all been battling sickness this week. I know it's the enemy."
- "My son has been so disobedient today. The enemy is really going after me."
- "I have been so distracted today. I know it's Satan trying to prevent me from getting this done."
- "This week has been full of aggravations. I attribute it to the enemy."
- "I lost my keys right as I was going out the door. I know that was Satan trying to prevent me from getting there."

Those statements sound to me like we give a lot more credit to the enemy than he deserves. And if you've ever found yourself saying or thinking those same things, consider the following:

- Satan is not omnipresent (as Christ is), meaning he can only be in one place at any given time. Do you really think he is wreaking the most havoc he can by constantly hanging out in *your* corner of the world, town, or building?
- We are capable of being distracted by any number of things, including an undisciplined, wandering mind. Many times our own negative thoughts can wreak enough havoc that Satan's influence isn't needed. Philippians 4:8 puts the burden on us to dwell on whatever is true, noble, right, pure, lovely, and admirable. Furthermore, 2 Corinthians 10:5 tells us to "demolish arguments and every pretension that sets itself up against the knowledge of God" and to "take captive every thought to make it obedient to Christ."

- We are fully capable of falling into temptation and sin without Satan's influence because of the weakness of our flesh and our failure to yield to Christ. As James 1:14 says, "Each person is tempted when they are dragged away by their own evil desire and enticed. Then, after desire has conceived, it gives birth to sin; and sin, when it is full-grown, gives birth to death."

Yes, we are told in the New Testament that "our struggle is not against flesh and blood, but against the rulers, against the authorities, against the powers of this dark world and against the spiritual forces of evil in the heavenly realms" (Ephesians 6:12).

However, Scripture also states that Christ is fully able to deter, demolish, and destroy any type of evil or provocation that might be launched against you (Hebrews 2:14). That power is not something reserved for Christ at some future time. It was given to Christ when He died on the cross for us (1 John 3:8).

So before you see yourself as defeated, think again: You are on the winning team. All power and authority, through Christ, is on your side.

God's Protective Power

Not only is God far more powerful than Satan, but ultimately, He must grant permission to Satan if he's going to try to mess with you.

> Nothing touches you that hasn't first gone through God's loving hands.

In the Old Testament story of Job, Satan had to ask permission to touch anything that Job had. He also had to gain specific permission from God to even touch Job's physical body and inflict harm on him in any way. And when God allowed the first two requests, Satan was specifically told he did not have permission to take Job's life. This makes it clear God is fully in control of when one's life ends. Satan can't inflict harm upon us without God's permission.

In the Gospels, Jesus Himself told Simon Peter, "Satan has demanded *permission* to sift you like wheat" (Luke 22:31 NASB). Why would Satan ask Jesus for permission to tempt His disciple? Wouldn't it be a much better strategy to launch a surprise attack on Peter so Jesus couldn't defend him? Satan wasn't just being polite. He *had* to ask permission to even go near Peter because Peter was in Christ's protective hand. Furthermore, in Jesus' prayer in John 17:12, note what He tells His heavenly Father: "While I was with them, I protected them and kept them safe." Later, in verse 15, Jesus said, "My prayer is not that you take them out of the world but that you protect them from the evil one." Then after Jesus died on the cross for us and conquered death through His resurrection from the grave, He made this promise as He ascended into heaven: "I am with you always" (Matthew 28:20; see also Hebrews 13:5).

Find Refuge in God

From the moment you and I turn our lives over to Christ and trust Him with our salvation, we are placed in God's protective care. So nothing touches you that hasn't first gone through His loving hands. With that kind of power—and that kind of protective love—in our corner, nothing should be able to shake us.

If you're going through something that hurts right now, your loving heavenly Father must see it as having an eternal benefit for you—that it will shape you and mold you into whom He designed you to be. And that means He has not, for a moment, lost control of the situation. Find comfort in that truth. And find your refuge in Him.

It is during the painful times of life that our faith is truly put to the test. And yes, there will be times when life isn't fair and we feel the rub. But God is sovereign over those times as well. Nowhere in Hannah's story do we hear of God's dealings in the life of Peninnah, nor in the lives of her children and the legacy they left. But we do hear of Hannah and the enduring legacy of her son, Samuel.

Trust God with *your* story and trust that He will care for you simply because you're His. To be able to walk tall and steady in spite of whatever is trying to wreak havoc on your life is to know, without a doubt, who is in control. Will you trust that God has you right where He wants you for whatever He has in mind?

Let Alena encourage your heart with these closing words:

"When I neared round two of chemo—the day of my fiftieth birthday—and I felt a fear that made my very being quake [because of how the chemo eventually killed her husband], God comforted me with His words in Isaiah 43:1-3:

> Fear not, for I have redeemed you; I have called you by your name, you are Mine. When you pass *through* the waters, I will be with you; and *through* the rivers, they shall not overflow you. When you walk *through* the fire, you shall not be burned, nor shall the flame scorch you. For I am the LORD your God, the Holy One of Israel, your Savior."

Whether your issue feels like deep water, a rushing river, or a blazing fire, God can certainly help you *through* whatever you are experiencing. So cling to Him. And let Him carry you through whatever lies ahead.

Trusting in the Power of His Protection

Read through the following passages of Scripture and write out who and what your defense is:

"The LORD will fight for you; you need only to be still" (Exodus 14:14).

Who is your defense?

What must you do?

"Do not be anxious about anything, but in every situation, by prayer and petition, with thanksgiving, present your requests to God. And the peace of God, which transcends all understanding, will guard your hearts and your minds in Christ Jesus" (Philippians 4:6-7).

What is your defense?

What must you do?

"What, then, shall we say in response to these things? If God is for us, who can be against us?" (Romans 8:31).

Who is your defense?

What must you do?

"I am convinced that neither death nor life, neither angels nor demons, neither the present nor the future, nor any powers, neither height nor depth, nor anything else in all creation, will be able to separate us from the love of God that is in Christ Jesus our Lord" (Romans 8:38-39).

What is your defense?

What must you do?

A Prayer in the Midst of Provocation

Lord God,

Thank You for knowing all about what harasses my heart. And thank You that You are stronger than anything that threatens to harm or intimidate me. Help me to cling to You and see You as my "refuge and strength, an ever-present help in trouble" (Psalm 46:1). I trust that You have been waiting to show Yourself strong on my behalf. I wait for You to come through in a mighty way for me.

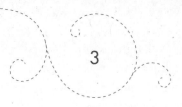

3

The Blind Spot

When Everyone Else Thinks You're Fine

> Her husband...would say to her, "...*why
> are you weeping? Why don't you eat?
> Why are you downhearted?* Don't I mean
> more to you than ten sons?"
>
> 1 Samuel 1:8

You know what it's like to go through life with a smile on your face even though you're hurting, don't you?

While others see only what's on the outside—which might appear polished and perfect—God sees your heart...and your tears.

And He wants *you* to see that He is all you truly need.

All her life, Ramona acted like everything was fine. But deep within her heart, she ached for more. She longed to experience a father's love.

Ramona had been abused by the only father she knew while growing up. When she was nine years old, her parents divorced. A few years later, she learned that the father she thought to be hers was really her stepfather.

"My mother started writing a book, and in order to protect me from finding out the truth through the book instead of directly from her, she told me a different man had been my birth father," Ramona said. "I was devastated when I found out my 'father' was really my stepfather and my mother knew nothing about my biological father.

I ended up saying, 'It's all right, Mom, I'll be okay.' But then I ran to my room and cried, knowing I was not okay.

"Feeling the father-loss and not knowing where to turn, I came to the Lord at age seventeen," Ramona said. When she understood that God loved her and sent His Son to die in her place to pay for her sins, it made a huge impact on her life. "For the first time ever I felt a love I had never known before, and for a little while, just knowing I was loved was my saving grace. The father-ache would show itself from time to time and I would bug my mom to tell me who my biological father was, but her answer was 'I don't know' or no answer at all."

"I remember telling God, 'You're the best Daddy a girl could have.'"

Ramona carried that longing to know her earthly father into her marriage. "When I got married I thought my husband would fill that void, but my expectation was too great and my marriage ended after thirty years."

Ramona remembers crying out to God for comfort, understanding, and deliverance from the pain while her marriage was crumbling.

"During my marriage, I put my husband on a pedestal. He became an idol in my life. At times I even looked to him as a father. But as the divorce proceeded, I realized I had to come back to my "first love," who is Jesus. When I did that, I began to see the many ways God was taking care of me as a father or husband would. He began showing up in the little things in life—He provided every bit of comfort I needed, every physical and financial need I had. He did it all one day at a time. He also put people in my life who encouraged and helped me through it all. Once I started seeing those little miracles happen, I started calling Him 'Daddy.' I remember telling God, 'You're the best Daddy a girl could have.'"

As Ramona went through her painful divorce, all the while

continuing to long for a father's love, everyone around her thought she was just fine.

That's the way it was for Hannah too.

Returning to Hannah's Story

Hannah's husband couldn't figure out why she was so unhappy at not being able to have a child. In 1 Samuel 1:8 we read, "Elkanah her husband said to her, 'Hannah, why do you weep and why do you not eat and why is your heart sad? Am I not better to you than ten sons?'" (NASB).

Okay, I know what you might be thinking. *Typical man! He really thinks his wife should be so elated that she has him for a husband that she doesn't feel pain in other areas of her life!* I don't think Elkanah meant to sound self-absorbed or overconfident in his ability to please his wife. However, remarks like his aren't helpful when a woman is hurting. Remarks like "Why isn't what you have right now good enough?" only cut deeper into a woman's heart, making her feel that no one understands her pain.

Could there be anything more insensitive or hurtful than when someone points out what you *do* have when you are honestly pouring out your heart about what hurts in your life? Hannah's husband wasn't able to comfort her with his words. In fact, his well-meaning comment could have been taken as insensitive and clueless. When a woman is staring at a void or feeling an ache in her heart, she needs someone to say, "I understand. And I'm hurting with you."

Refusing to Settle

I'm sure you've heard some of these well-intentioned comments yourself:

"At least you *have* a husband."

"At least you *already have* a child."

"You may not enjoy it, but at least you *have* a job."

"Well, at least you're healthy."

"At least you still have _____."

"At least you don't suffer with _____."

Oh, the sting of well-intentioned remarks. And oh, the sting of those two guilt-ridden words: "At least…"

As I've ministered to women over the past 30 years, I have met quite a few who settled for "at least" in their life. And yet I believe that if God went to such great extremes to show His love for you and me by having His only Son die on the cross for us, then He did not intend for us to be content with "at least."

Yes, God's Word says we are to be thankful "in all circumstances" (1 Thessalonians 5:18). It also tells us that "godliness with *contentment* is great gain" (1 Timothy 6:6). But God doesn't want our gratitude and contentment to be a form of resignation ("I guess I should be happy with this, since it's all I will ever get anyway"). Rather, God wants His children to be full of anticipation for the "more" that He is so capable of giving—to the point that we thank Him ahead of time for all that He is about to do. This God who tells us to be thankful in all things actually raises the bar when we decide to settle for less or *at least* what life brings us.

In Ephesians 3:20, we are told that God "is able to do *exceedingly abundantly above* all that we ask or think, according to the power that works in us" (NKJV). You and I often hear or think or say the words "at least" when it comes to our lives. And yet God's Word says:

- "If you believe, you will receive whatever you ask for in prayer" (Matthew 21:22).

- "Ask and you will receive, so that your joy may be made full" (John 16:24 NASB).

- He "is able to do immeasurably more than all we ask or imagine, according to his power that is at work within us" (Ephesians 3:20).

- "Without faith it is impossible to please God" (Hebrews 11:6).

Those words, my friend, come from a God who is not stingy, and who doesn't bow out after He's done the very minimum in your life. He is, instead, the God who says, "If you, then, though you are evil, know how to give good gifts to your children, how much more will your Father in heaven give good gifts to those who ask him!" (Matthew 7:11).

Hannah could have hung her head in shame and said, "Elkanah, you're right. You are good to me. Who am I to want more than a husband who loves me? I will give up this dream for a child and face reality. Apparently God doesn't want me to be a mom after all."

Yes, Hannah could have said that and, although it sounds humble, grateful, and almost spiritual, it also sounds faithless. Hannah would have been giving up, throwing in the towel, conceding to her circumstances rather than believing God could answer her plea.

When Abraham's wife, Sarah, laughed and doubted that God could give her a child in her old age, the Angel of the Lord rebuked her by saying straight-out to Abraham, "Is anything too hard for the LORD?" (Genesis 18:14). Maybe those words echoed in Hannah's ears, giving her hope, even though she was being told that she had enough. Hannah was still of child-bearing age. Her situation wouldn't even take a miracle, as Sarah's situation did. Hannah must have known that God is still the Giver of every good gift and the One who could make anything possible. As we will see in the next chapter, Hannah chose to pour her heart out to God and ask Him for the "immeasurably more" that she was hoping for.

Perhaps those words from the Angel of the Lord ("Is anything too hard for the Lord?") need to echo in *our* ears too each time we begin to think, *Why should I even pray for this? What are the odds of this happening? Maybe I should be happy that at least…*

Believing Him for More

You and I have our reasons for not coming to God and pouring out our hearts. Sometimes it's because we feel guilty about asking God for something. Other times it's because we don't believe that He would want to bless our lives or we feel we don't deserve anything more from Him. When you and I say, "I don't deserve any more than I have right now," we are actually correct in our assumption, because God doesn't give us good gifts because we *deserve* them. He gives us good gifts because He is good and compassionate and wants to bless His children.

So don't fall into the mind-set of saying, "I don't believe God can or will give me any more," or "I don't deserve more than what I already have." Instead, remember that God loves to bless His children. Don't be reluctant to pour out your heart to Him. Rather than settle for the *least* in your life, allow for the possibility God may want to do "immeasurably more than all [you] ask or imagine" (Ephesians 3:20).

Ramona's Search

Ramona chose to hope for more too. It was the desire of her heart to find her biological father, so when her mother passed away, Ramona decided she would try to find him on her own. God knew this was on Ramona's heart, and He appeared to divinely orchestrate the process as it unfolded.

Ramona sought the help of a website aimed at helping people trace their genealogies and locate lost relatives. She took a DNA test and submitted the results in the hopes of finding lost relatives and, among them, her biological father. In the meantime, a woman named Becky, who had been adopted at birth, was also searching the site for lost relatives. Becky had found her biological father and family, which included her biological father's twin brother. When Becky discovered through DNA tests that Ramona had a 98 percent chance of being her first or second cousin and she was looking for her biological father too, Becky decided to help Ramona in her search.

After some investigating, Becky discovered that her uncle (her biological father's twin brother) was Ramona's biological father. (A further DNA test proved that this man was, indeed, Ramona's father.) Ramona and her biological father communicated for six months by telephone and through letters. Then Ramona flew to a family reunion to meet her father, Becky, and other relatives.

At first Ramona's heart exuded with joy. She didn't think it was any coincidence that, as she began to trust wholeheartedly in God as her heavenly Father, He restored to her an earthly father as well. She felt her life was finally complete.

But Ramona soon learned that she had put more hope in this earthly father than she had intended. Because she had been without a father for so long, and had in some ways idolized the role of a father, she had extremely high expectations for this man she had never known during childhood. She found herself, at times, like a little girl trying to make up for what she never experienced during her childhood. She struggled for weeks with what to do next now that she knew who her father was. Today she fears her expectations and her desire for a closer relationship with him pushed him away. And now she finds that—although she knows who her father is and her dream of meeting him has come true—the tears still fall.

"Because I'm human, I had certain expectations of what I wanted to happen with this new relationship," Ramona said. "But I found out that I had to take it slower than I wanted and that it didn't go exactly as I had hoped or planned. I had to leave it in God's hands and rest in the fact that He knows best about relationships."

At one time, Ramona thought that finding her father would clear up her "blind spot" and help her to see life more clearly. Instead, it exposed a blind spot she already had. She had put her earthly father in the role that only God can fill. Today Ramona is not as close with her biological father as she had hoped to become. And yet she finds comfort knowing that her *real* father is her heavenly Father, who will never leave her, let her down, or disappoint her in any way.

"I've always known the missing piece in my life was not having a father as I was growing up. I always felt like half of a person. I knew God had loved me all along, and until this year, I didn't realize how much He did. And today, even though I have found my biological father, God is still the best Daddy any girl could have."

When Ramona asked God for "more," she was given the knowledge of who her father is. But she also gained with it the experience of knowing that no person or experience this side of heaven will be able to fully satisfy or complete her. Ramona continues to give the broken pieces of her life to the Lord, who continues to fill those holes with Himself. Today, Ramona will tell you that she has received God's "immeasurably more" through what He allowed her to learn about His unconditional, ever-present, sacrificial love for her as a Father.

What's Your Blind Spot?

Too often we assume our blind spot is the pain we are experiencing, and that everything would be clearer and better once the pain is gone. But frequently the *real* blind spot is the work God wants to do in us—a work we don't see taking shape yet.

Are you still longing for a husband? Perhaps your blind spot is the realization that God wants to be your provider-husband and pour into your life the love you've always longed for.

Are you longing for a child to hold in your arms? Perhaps your blind spot is the realization that God wants to fill that place of longing in your heart with Himself alone.

> God understands the longings of your heart even more than you do.

Are you hoping for healing of childhood wounds? It's possible God wants you to see Him as the perfect Father who is able to make you complete and whole.

Are you disappointed because you haven't been able to fulfill a specific dream? Maybe God wants to show you that when you pursue Him with all your heart, you will be living out His dream for you.

God understands the longings of your heart even more than you do. He knows what is at the root of everything you desire. And when He becomes your ultimate longing, He will either grant your desire because He knows you can finally handle what it is you are asking for, or you will come to realize that you have no desire for anything but Him alone.

Just months ago, Ramona believed her testimony was the story of how God became her heavenly Father and allowed her to find her earthly father. She was so excited about being able to tell a story with a happy ending. That story made sense. And it made her happy. And while it's true that God engineered the circumstances for her to find her biological father, she now sees that there is so much more to her story. She now understands the greater transformation that God wanted to do in her—to show her that He is the only One who satisfies and that nothing this side of heaven will be able to fill her as He can. She now knows, through experience, that God's love for her can never be compared to anything she can find on this earth. She now looks for nothing else in addition to Him. God alone is her prize.

When God Touches Our Blind Spot

We read in Scripture of Jesus healing a man who was blind from birth. And we discover three very interesting things in the story— why the man was blind, how he was healed, and how he responded to his newfound sight.

Follow the story with me from John chapter 9 (and notice the parts I've italicized for emphasis):

> As [Jesus] went along, he saw a man blind from birth.
> His disciples asked him, "Rabbi, who sinned, this man
> or his parents, that he was born blind?" "Neither this

man nor his parents sinned," said Jesus, "but *this hap-pened so that the works of God might be displayed in him…*"

After saying this, *he spit on the ground, made some mud with the saliva, and put it on the man's eyes.* "Go," he told him, "wash in the Pool of Siloam" (this word means "Sent"). So the man went and washed, and came home seeing…

They brought to the Pharisees the man who had been blind. Now the day on which Jesus had made the mud and opened the man's eyes was a Sabbath. Therefore the Pharisees also asked him how he had received his sight. "He put mud on my eyes," the man replied, "and I washed, and now I see." Some of the Pharisees said, "This man is not from God, for he does not keep the Sabbath." But others asked, "How can a sinner perform such signs?" So they were divided…

A second time they summoned the man who had been blind. "Give glory to God by telling the truth," they said. "We know this man [Jesus] is a sinner [because He healed the man on the Sabbath]." He replied, "Whether he is a sinner or not, I don't know. *One thing I do know. I was blind but now I see!*" (verses 1-3,6-7,13-16,24-25).

From this story we can glean the following insights:

1. It's possible our "blind spot" exists so that God may be glorified through us.

In responding to the disciples' question about whose sin was responsible for the blind man's condition, Jesus pointed out that the man's blindness was not the result of sin in his or his parents' lives. It was so that God could be glorified by Jesus healing him. Think about that for a moment. Might the "blind spot" in your life (a health problem, the absence of someone or something you long for, or an area of your life you think needs to be healed or fixed) exist so that Christ can do a glorifying work in you?

2. God's method of healing is sometimes unconventional—or uncomfortable.

In this story we find that Jesus "spit on the ground, made some mud with the saliva, and put it on the man's eyes" (verse 6). Now I don't know about you, but I wouldn't want someone to spit in some dirt and put mud in my eyes. How weird. How uncomfortable. How unsanitary. Couldn't Jesus have just said, "See" and the man would've had eyesight? Of course. But Jesus wanted this man to obey Him by going to the pool and washing off. And He wanted him to trust Him through the process He was taking him through.

Can you imagine what might have been going through that man's mind as he walked—or felt around as he stumbled, perhaps—to the Pool of Siloam? He might have been thinking, *I sure hope this works, or I'm really going to look like a fool.* Or maybe he thought, *Is this all? Just make it to the pool and wash? I can do this!* I'd like to think that he was full of excitement at the anticipation of seeing for the very first time in his life: *God, get me safely and quickly to this pool so that my eyes will be opened and I can tell everyone what You have done!*

God may decide to take you through a process as He heals your hurt. For Ramona, not knowing her biological father was painful. But once she found him and realized they wouldn't have the kind of family relationship she had hope for, she learned to trust the process God had taken her through to heal her heart and show her that He is the only Father who will never disappoint.

3. When we can finally "see," our declaration is simple.

The Pharisees were asking this formerly blind man all sorts of questions. They looked and sounded intimidating, I'm sure. But his answer to them was brief and clear: "One thing I do know. I was blind but now I see!" I love the simplicity of this man's declaration—his testimony, his account of what Jesus did. And isn't that the story of every one of us when God gets a hold of our lives and shows us the truth? "I may not have all the answers, but one thing I do know: I was blind and now I see."

Ramona recently emailed me with the latest update of God's healing in her life:

"I finally got my reality check. I found my dad. I have a dad, but it goes no further than that. It would be another miracle if it did, but it doesn't. What we have, we have, so I have let go of all my expectations for that relationship and continue to praise God that I still have His love and attention 24/7. I've known rejection all my life, and this time I accept the rejection knowing I have something better in the Lord."

Like the blind man who received his sight, Ramona now sees, for the first time, and is able to declare: "One thing I do know. I thought I was fatherless, but I'm not."

For years, Ramona believed that finding her father would be the magical element that would make her feel complete. Yet today she sees that what she really needed all along was to trust wholeheartedly in her heavenly Father's love for her. God showed her that she already had all she longed for. She just didn't realize it. God gave sight to her blind spot.

Finding Your Sight

What is *your* blind spot? What are you longing for so much that it is blinding you from seeing God? Take that intense longing to Jesus. As you begin to seek Him above everything else, your eyes will be opened to the truth of who He is. He is not just the One who knows you and hears you and sees you. He is the One who *frees* you too.

Our Savior meant it when He said, "You will know the truth, and the truth will set you free" (John 8:32 NLT).

Giving Sight to Your Blind Spot

Take some time to respond to these questions (in prayer or by writing your responses below):

1. What have you been longing for, and how might God use that longing to show you something more about Himself?

2. The blind man's simple statement (or story) was: "One thing I do know. I was blind but now I see!" (John 9:25). Ramona's simple statement is: "I thought I was fatherless, but I'm not."

   What is *your* simple statement to describe what God has done (or is doing) in your life?

A Prayer for Clearer Vision

God,

How I long to see what You want me to see right now. I know how I want You to fix or heal situations in my life. And yet You have so much more that You want for me than what I am merely asking. I believe You really can do immeasurably more in and through my life. So would You help me to trust You for the "more" You are waiting to accomplish? I trust You, no matter how uncomfortable or unconventional Your process might be. I truly want to see clearly…and I want to be set free.

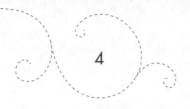

4

Pouring It Out

When You Finally Get Desperate

She, greatly distressed, *prayed to the LORD and wept bitterly.*

1 SAMUEL 1:10 (NASB)

Have you ever felt absolutely desperate before God?

Desperate for His grace? Desperate for His healing? Desperate for His help and intervention so you don't keep making a mess of things?

Michele has been there.

And it wasn't easy for her to get to the place where she could pour out her heart to God and share her story with others.

She contacted me after I spoke at the women's retreat hosted by her church. She felt like the wayward woman of the group that weekend, with a bottle of wine stashed away for her trip home and a heart full of secrets she didn't want anyone to know about.

But God broke her during the weekend and pressed on her heart that it's never too late—and she's never too messed up—to pour it all out before God and seek His restoration.

"At the end of retreat, when no one was there by the podium, I finally went forward and got vulnerable with God on my knees," Michele told me in an email. "He met me there. It was messy. I finally cried, bawled, got angry with God, and then asked Him to redeem me again."

The key word being *again*.

Michele, like so many women, struggles with a pattern of addiction, repentance, a new start, loving life, slipping up, feeling guilty, and then starting the cycle all over again. *Doesn't God get tired of hearing it? Isn't enough enough with Him?* she wonders at times.

And yet she's not alone. We all ask the same questions from time to time. Each of us, in one way or another, has our cycles of sin. Our addictions. Our good days, our not-so-good days, and our absolutely ugly days. We all have a dark side we don't like to come face-to-face with. We all so desperately need God. We need Him to hear us, see us, and meet us in our tears.

When Michele, a woman who rarely cries, finally got real with God, He met her there and gave her hope once again.

Michele was in an abusive 12-year marriage. She had two children with her husband before legally separating from him for their protection. He then divorced her. Life hasn't necessarily been easier since then.

"There is no justice on this earth, nor in court," she said. "Perpetrators get away with it. I live with it. I'm ill from it because I rarely cry. I'm also addicted to opiates now. Sometimes a pill—or two—or three—will make things feel better. My testimony is tremendous and if I am ever fully healed again, it could greatly be used for God's glory, I am sure."

We each have a story that eventually brings us to our knees before God. But that, my friend, is the day our tears become most precious to Him. So precious, that Scripture says He stores our tears in a bottle. Why would God collect our tears? Because they come at a cost to us. And because He loves us. Because He will not waste them. Because tears poured out in repentance, in pain, in search of restoration become part of our heavenly Father's precious possession. They become something He can redeem and restore.

"I thought my tears were ugly," Michele said, referring to her battle with God alone that day after the women's retreat. "Because I let the ugly come out when I cry, that is why I do it alone. It was really ugly, messy, mascara everywhere, snotty, fists angrily in the air asking, 'Why?' But then I was humbly, softly begging for His touch because though I get angry at God, and myself and men, I still want to feel unconditionally loved by God and able to love myself again and then maybe be able to trust a man in order to fall in love someday and maybe be married again."

Oh the cries of an honest woman's heart before God.

Michele received God's restoration once again and is taking life one day at a time.

Releasing the Tears

Personal, inner turmoil is one situation that leads us to pour out our hearts to God in prayer. We can find relief when we confess our sins, as Michele did, and ask Him to restore our lives again. God offers us restoration, redemption, and relief as we pour out our hearts to Him. Sometimes, though, we end up coming to God completely depleted because of the circumstances that are happening all around us. That's how it was for Gayla. She felt overwhelmed and helpless on account of the pain and suffering that took the lives of three women very close to her.

In the span of a few short years, Gayla, a pastor's wife at a large church in Colorado, lost three precious women in her life.

First, she and her husband, Tim, lost both of their fathers. Then Gayla's mom was diagnosed with Alzheimer's disease at the age of 82.

"I saw God working in so many ways...But not in the divine healing way."

"My mom was always my best and closest friend. Her encouragement and wisdom through the years helped me greatly in being a wife, a mother, and in full-time ministry for over 30 years," Gayla said. So it was heartwrenching for Gayla to see her mother decline for seven years before passing away at the age of 89.

"Every year during those seven years she grew worse," Gayla said. "Even though the Lord led me to a wonderful home to place her in for twenty-four-hour-care, it was still an agonizing decision."

During the first year of her mother's placement, Debbie—a close friend of Gayla's—was diagnosed with cancer and lived only two more years after her diagnosis.

"Also, during the second year of my mom's illness, my mother-in-law's health declined. She too had to be placed in assisted living," Gayla said. "All three of these women were strong believers and had led righteous, godly lives. Daily prayers and fasting became the norm for me and many other prayer warriors, yet it seemed to be of no avail. We didn't get our prayers answered the way we had hoped."

While Gayla was praying for healing in these women's lives, or for some assurance that their situations would improve, she never saw it happen.

"I saw God working in so many ways" Gayla said. "But not in the divine healing way.

"During these hard years, we never had a good report or saw anything get better for our moms or my friend. It was agonizing and caused my faith to be challenged. This was extremely difficult while being in full-time ministry and leading a flock of people. It was heart-wrenching as mom and my mother-in-law declined and Debbie got worse. However, I witnessed God's sustaining grace. It wasn't the answer I looked for, but He was still keeping all of them in the palm of His hand."

Gayla admits there were times when the loss in her life seemed more than she could bear.

"When in despair, I packed my bags to leave and run on numerous occasions, but the Lord would always send someone to stop me and reason with me, or I would hear a sermon that would break the chains of despair and unbelief. Also, God brought people to me who needed counsel and prayer when I was at my worst. This was confusing to me—why God would have me pour out my life to others

when I so needed others to pour themselves into me. Yet I saw what
He was doing. I learned how to give in extreme pain and how to let
His Spirit speak through a broken vessel. Even when I didn't think I
believed anymore, the Spirit in me was stronger than my flesh and
would go into overdrive to enable me to minister to others. These
were big life lessons from the Lord, and I truly learned that 'when I
am weak, He is strong.'"

Gayla's life lessons were the essence of what the apostle Paul
wrote about in 2 Corinthians 12:9-10:

> He said to me, "My grace is sufficient for you, for my
> power is made perfect in weakness." Therefore I will
> boast all the more gladly about my weaknesses, so that
> Christ's power may rest on me. That is why, for Christ's
> sake, I delight in weaknesses, in insults, in hardships, in
> persecutions, in difficulties. For when I am weak, then
> I am strong.

Turning Toward Him

Gayla not only received strength from God in her sorrow and
weakness, but she learned during that dark time what it really
means to cry out to God in desperation. And she learned that while
God wasn't giving her what she was asking for, He was giving her
Himself.

"His answer to me was that He is sovereign and He has a plan
for my life that doesn't always make sense. His ways are higher and
very different from mine (Isaiah 55:8-9). He sometimes puts us in
uncomfortable places. In the beginning, the sorrows of these places
cause deep pain and create anguish.

"Screaming, crying, and feeling alone won't change anything. I
had to learn the hard way to run to His Word daily, and find Him
for the peace to face each day—not for a week, not for a month, but
for *several years*. I learned (and often *still* learn) to not turn toward

the pain, the injustice, or the questions, but to turn toward *Him*! This is not easy.

"My flesh wants to feel better and have things 'normal.' But God keeps us wrapped in the dark cocoon so our only option is to turn to Him—and nothing or no one else—until we are truly strong enough to emerge as a butterfly. And guess what? Life doesn't look the same when we emerge. 'Normal' is now on God's terms. I never would have thought after knowing the Lord and working in His kingdom for 30 years that I would have to learn it at this level. I think as Christians we don't expect to face this level of brokenness because we know how to avoid sin and its effects. But we live in a broken world, and we still encounter the effects of that."

Hannah's Heartfelt Prayer

What does it look like to pour out our hearts in prayer, desperate for God's ear?

For Gayla, it looked sometimes like darkness and silence, yet with a quiet assurance that God was present and listening.

For Michele, it looked messy and snotty and angry, and then tender.

For Hannah, it probably looked like a little of both.

When we envision Hannah pulling herself together and finding a quiet place to spend time alone with God, we tend to imagine a serene, peaceful woman quietly pouring out her heart to God. But I wonder if the scene was more the opposite.

Scripture does not imply that Hannah's prayer was a self-controlled whispering that only God heard. Rather, the passage says she was "in bitterness of soul," and "wept in anguish" as she prayed to the Lord (1 Samuel 1:10 NKJV). The original Hebrew text here implies anger and sobbing.[1] As one translation states, Hannah was "crushed in spirit" and "cried and cried—inconsolably."[2]

Hannah's prayer was a heap of frustration, anger, sorrow, deep disappointment, and grief that she laid in front of God without reservation.

Furthermore, Scripture doesn't make us guess the words of her prayer. Rather, we are told what she said amidst those tears. One paraphrase describes her prayer this way:

> Crushed in soul, Hannah prayed to GOD and cried and cried—inconsolably. Then she made a vow:
>
> Oh, GOD-of-the-Angel-Armies,
> If you'll take a good, hard look at my pain,
> If you'll quit neglecting me and
>   go into action for me
> By giving me a son,
> I'll give him completely, unreservedly to you.
> I'll set him apart for a life of holy discipline
>   (verses 10-11 MSG).

God heard that prayer, deal and all, and granted Hannah's request. But before we look at her "deal" in the next chapter, and her commitment to follow through in response to God answering her prayer, I want to look at *how* Hannah prayed—and how it relates to where *you* are in your frustration, bitterness, sorrow, or deep disappointment.

How Hannah Prayed

Look at Scripture's description of how Hannah prayed:

> As she kept on praying to the LORD, Eli observed her mouth. Hannah was praying in her heart, and her lips were moving but her voice was not heard. Eli thought she was drunk and said to her, "How long are you going to stay drunk? Put away your wine."
>
> "Not so, my lord," Hannah replied, "I am a woman who is deeply troubled. I have not been drinking wine or beer; I was pouring out my soul to the LORD. Do not take your servant for a wicked woman; I have been praying here out of my great anguish and grief" (1 Samuel 1:12-16).

Now it's one thing to pray silently with your mouth moving. It's quite another to look drunk! And for Eli, the priest, to believe Hannah was intoxicated, she must have been doing more than just mouthing her words. She must have been impassioned and giving the appearance that she was under the control of something else. She did say, after all, that she was praying "out of my great anguish and grief."

Have you ever prayed that way? So impassioned that you are completely given over to what you are praying for? "Enough, God. I can't take this anymore. I am desperate for Your intervention. Do something, because I can't live like this anymore!"

And are you in a desperate place right now, like Hannah, where you're ready to make a deal with God?

"Lord, just give me what I want and I'll do anything You ask."

"God, please give me a baby and I'll give him back to you like Hannah did."

"Lord, please let me have a husband and I'll never ask for anything again."

"God, please take away this pain or take me home with You because I don't want to go on anymore the way life is right now."

Sometimes we can be so focused on what we want that we're willing to do *anything* to get it. God sees that kind of desperation too. And He doesn't take it lightly.

Ecclesiastes 5:5 tells us, "It is better not to make a vow than to make one and not fulfill it." Hannah, apparently, knew the seriousness of making her vow and she didn't do it hastily or without thinking it over. She had cried, refused to eat, and heard her husband try to talk "sense" into her. Then she pulled herself together, ate, and *then* slipped away to pour out her heart to God. Keep in mind too that Hannah's predicament had already gone on "year after year." It had been a long process of pain. She was at her wit's end. And she was ready to do whatever it took for God to hear her and grant her request.

In our words today, her prayer might have sounded like this:

> God, I'm serious…now more than I've ever been. I want this *so* much. But now I want it for *You*. If You'll give me a son, I'll give him back to You all the days of his life. He will be with *You* more than he will be with me. But that doesn't matter because it's not about me anymore. I want him for *Your* purposes. And I want *You* to be pleased with my request.

I want you to notice a few things about Hannah's heartfelt "deal" with God.

1. She was specific in her request. Hannah's request was, "If you give me a *son*…" She didn't say, "Whatever You can do, God, would be fine." She laid her request on the line very specifically. Are you ready to be specific with God in requesting exactly what you want?

2. She showed faith in her request. Hannah told the Lord her part of the deal should He grant her request. That tells me she was asking in faith, believing He would answer. In Mark 9:17-27, a man asked Jesus to heal his demon-possessed son by saying, "If you can do anything, take pity on us and help us." How did Jesus respond? He looked at the man squarely in the eyes and said "*If* you can?" In other words, "You're coming to Me and asking Me for something and you're not even sure I can do it?" Then Jesus said "Everything is possible for one who believes." The man then responded, with the utmost honesty: "I do believe; help me overcome my unbelief!" God wants us to ask Him in faith, trusting that He knows the best response for us.

3. She was surrendered in her request. "If you give me a son, I will give him back to you." Devout Israelite parents were expected to commit their firstborn son to the Lord, a requirement of the Mosaic

> God wants us to ask Him in faith, trusting that He knows the best response for us.

Law (Exodus 22:29). Hannah went further in her prayer, though. She appeared to be making a Nazirite vow (although she never used the word *Nazirite*) for her son—which included abstaining from cutting one's hair or drinking any fermented beverage for a specified time in order to be set apart for God (Numbers 6:2-7). Interestingly, no other incidents of the taking of this vow on behalf of someone else are found in the Bible.[3] By offering to give her hoped-for son back to God, Hannah was demonstrating her realization that what she asked for and received was God's anyway. Therein lies the principle to keep in mind with *anything* we ask of God.

What if you and I had that perspective with regard to everything we have, and everything we ask for? Maybe we'd ask for less. Maybe we'd ask for more. In either case, our prayers might look altogether different.

When God Appears Not to Hear

I've heard many women say that they can't get to the point of "pouring out" in prayer because it feels like their prayers are bouncing off the ceiling.

We all have times when we pray and it feels like we're not connecting with God. There could be a few reasons for that. One reason could be that we are not in a relationship with God. (You may want to read "How to Know You Are God's Child" on page 193 for assurance that you are in a relationship with Him.) Another reason might be unconfessed sin in your life. If you are living in disobedience to God, you cannot expect Him to heed your requests. But if you've examined your life and know in your heart you are right before Him, perhaps God is allowing you to walk through a silent valley so you can sense His presence in the quiet, and not necessarily His words in the chaos.

Alena (from chapter 2), who saw cancer take her husband's life and then show up in her body, says: "Since I've been there, wondering at times if God has heard me, I do know now that even when it's silent He hears me. Keep crying out, don't let go of Him. He does hear you. Be real with Him and completely willing to hear what He wants to do in your life. Listen for the God moments.

"There are God moments every day for me. Something happens and I know, beyond a doubt, that God was behind it. And I think, *That was Him. He did that!*"

Our being able to recognize God at work in our lives is just one way we receive assurance that He hasn't forgotten us when all is silent. And even when we just aren't sure, we need to keep the channels of communication open so that it's easier for us to pray when tragedy strikes or discouragement flares up.

Sometimes, however, it's our own doubt telling us that God doesn't hear us, and we need to counter that with faith in God's Word and His promise to hear us (1 John 5:14-15). We also need to make sure we don't become complacent in our prayer life and fall into a pattern of "talking" but not really "listening" to Him. So when we feel our prayers are bouncing off the ceiling, rather than give up in resignation, those are the times we need to persevere and "push through" that ceiling with impassioned prayer.

Now, if you're gauging whether or not God hears your prayers by whether or not He has given you what you've asked, that isn't a fair gauge. God's presence is there. He hears everything. But *how* He responds to your specific request is an altogether different matter.

Is it possible that God is not answering your prayer because you have attached strings to your request?

There are many people who pray for things and halfheartedly tell God they'll honor Him if He will first honor them:

Give me this job, God, and I'll go back to church.

God, find me a husband, then I'll serve You again.

God, make my career successful, then I'll start giving more money to Your causes.

I can't tell you how many times my husband, as a pastor, has heard someone say, "Pastor, pray that I get this job and then I'll be more faithful at coming to church," or "Pastor, please pray that I get this raise, because then I will be able to give more money to the church." My patient husband has even heard, "Pastor, pray that I win the lottery this weekend. I promise I'll give half of my winnings to the church!" (And those requests were made in all seriousness!) Would you believe that every time we've seen one of those "strings-attached prayer requests" answered favorably (and not from my husband's prayers, I'm pretty sure), the person who got the job or the promotion or the raise never showed up again? (In case you're wondering, we've never yet seen God say yes to anyone's prayers to win the lottery!)

Have you ever considered that God wants us to ask Him for what *He* wants to give us?

If a person is not giving God his time, priority, or money now, then he isn't going to start doing it when God blesses him with more. Besides, have you ever considered that God wants us to ask Him for what *He* wants to give us? (We'll look at that more in chapter 7.)

Gaining a New Perspective

It isn't just our dependence and persistent prayer God is after. He wants to see in us a desire for Him to use whatever *He* gives us—for *His* glory and renown. Second Chronicles 16:9 says, "The eyes of the LORD move to and fro throughout the earth that He may strongly support those whose heart is completely His" (NASB).

Remember when King Solomon asked God for wisdom? God came to Solomon and said, in essence, "Ask for whatever you want, and it's yours." Thankfully, Solomon chose wisdom—he wanted to know how to govern God's people wisely. As a result, God was pleased to give Solomon not only wisdom, but a whole lot more—all because Solomon's heart was aimed at pleasing God.

When Michele poured out her heart, as we saw earlier in this chapter, God met her in her desire to glorify Him, and He restored her life and her service to Him.

When Gayla poured out her heart, God didn't provide healing for the women in her life. But He enabled her to minister to others more deeply because of the brokenness she experienced.

So sometimes God's answer is yes, and other times it is no. *How* He responds is up to Him. In His perfect love and wisdom, He knows what is right and best for us. We're called to pray…and to trust Him. And when we do pray, we should do so with a desire to give back to God whatever it is He gives to us.

How Should We Pray?

We see from Hannah's story that she wept bitterly and cried out to God—and He heard her. One Bible commentator says Hannah stood out during her day because of her sincerity in prayer. Her "sadness of heart and persistence in prayer contrasted sharply with the prevalent corruption in worship led by Eli's sons (1 Samuel 2:12-17)."[4] How do you stand apart in your persistent prayer or longing?

Scripture tells us, "During the days of Jesus' life on earth, he offered up prayers and petitions with fervent cries and tears to the one who could save him from death, and he was heard because of his reverent submission" (Hebrews 5:7). This verse makes us think of Jesus' prayer in the Garden of Gethsemane, just before He was arrested and carried off to be crucified for the sins of the world. Scripture tells us that Jesus sweated blood and tears as He prayed. Can you imagine the intensity of that kind of prayer? Do we even know what it's like to feel so deeply about something in prayer that we sweat blood?

To the contrary, I think all too often we find ourselves on the opposite end of the spectrum when it comes to our prayers. We tend to feel so little. And we tend to "pray it safe."

I remember praying earnestly for God's leading as I was hoping to get my first publishing contract. I knew, beyond any doubt, that God had called me to write. I had received the affirmations over and over. I was just in that long, difficult, waiting period…waiting on God for His timing, which frequently seems a little slower than ours. "Please pray that my book proposal gets accepted. Please pray that this is it," I found myself saying to a good friend.

Her reply was, "I will pray for it if it's God's will." I knew what she was saying. Of course she wanted God's will for me; so did I. But years earlier, God's will for me to write had already been established and confirmed. I wonder sometimes if people sometimes respond that way so they don't have to pray for something specific *just in case it doesn't happen*. We can sometimes use "God's will" as our loophole. After all, no one wants to pray for something that ultimately doesn't happen. We like *successful* prayer. We like praying for tangible, specific things only if we believe those things are actually attainable. But that isn't faith.

I honestly believe we find specific, faith-building prayer too difficult. Or at minimum, we're hesitant to pray in that way. If what we pray for isn't answered in the way we had hoped, we fear that we might look like we were doubting, or we weren't obedient, or we weren't sincere in our prayers.

It's only as we cultivate intimacy with God that we will begin to see and share His heart for whatever it is we are asking for. While we might start out praying for something specific, over time, that specific request may change. For example, instead of praying, "God, help me get this book contract," my prayer had changed to "God, please do the work in me that You desire so that I can produce the book that will glorify You." There's a whole lot more of Him in that prayer than me. And that may be why He eventually answered it. God keeps me in balance as the tool to which He can and will receive glory, at His prerogative.

I now wish that the request I had posed to my friend had been "Please pray for God's work in me as I wait for His timing in all of this." That too, would have been a specific, tangible prayer. And it would have been a way of praying God's will for me instead of merely hoping for God to answer in a certain way.

What Are You Waiting For?

Before we leave this chapter, it's important to understand that in Hannah's life—and in yours—God is the One who has control over what is missing and what we so badly want. Just as "the Lord had closed her womb" and was preparing Hannah for a time in her life when she would come to Him in desperate prayer, He is in control over whatever has driven you to Him as well. He can provide at any time what it is you so badly desire. But if He hasn't answered your prayer, either He knows you don't need it as much you think you do, or He is developing in you a dependence on Him and a desperation for Him that you wouldn't cultivate if you got what you wanted as soon as you asked. Still another possibility is that He is preparing you for the time that He will give you what you are asking for.

No matter what happens, pour out your heart to Him, my friend. He hears you. And chances are, He's been waiting for you to ask for exactly what *He* wants to give.

Gaining Confidence in Prayer

Read the following verses and record here what they say about how we should pray:

1 John 5:14-15—

Matthew 21:22—

Philippians 4:6—

A Prayer of Transparency

Lord God,

You know what it is that I desire more than anything. And I know You want that place in my life. So would You help me to put You first and have the same desires for me that You do? Give me Your heart and Your longings. Help me to deeply care about what You care about. And help me to be willing to give back to You what my heart longs for. I long for Your purposes to be accomplished in and through my life. So have Your way with me and all that I have and don't have. I'm ready for You to change my life.

5

Sudden Backfire
When the Unthinkable Happens

Do not take your servant for a wicked woman;
I have been praying here out of my great anguish and grief.

1 SAMUEL 1:16

Amanda's life and marriage were finally headed in the direction she had hoped.

Jaman, her husband, was an energetic 29-year-old pastor who had just agreed to take a sabbatical and spend more time with his wife and 2½-year-old daughter, Belle. There were new possibilities on the horizon, and they were looking forward to receiving whatever direction God would give them for Jaman's personal life and ministry.

It was then, on the brink of a new chapter in life, that the unthinkable happened.

Early on a Saturday morning, May 19, 2012, Amanda was awakened by this text message: "Is everything ok? I just heard the news." The message was followed by a knock on the front door. When Amanda opened the door she saw two chaplains (the copastors of her church), and two church members. The four of them looked indescribably shocked. One of them had started to cry.

"Amanda, there's been an accident," one of them said. "Your husband has been shot."

They took Amanda to the hospital, where she discovered that

Jaman had been pronounced dead upon arrival. Amanda would soon learn that it wasn't an "accident" at all.

An alleged mentally ill woman who had reportedly been stalking Pastor Jaman and resented his positive influence on her family—some of whom were longtime attenders of his church—went to the church early that morning looking to kill him. Although Jaman wasn't supposed to be there that morning, and no one knew he would be, she asked for him, and shot him at point-blank range as soon as she saw him. Jaman had only enough time to push open a door (that eyewitnesses said was locked from the inside, by the way), run up a couple of steps, and stumble out onto the grass, where he collapsed into the arms of an ER chaplain who happened to be in the parking lot and rushed to his side. The chaplain later reported to Amanda that she was able to witness Jaman's last few moments, during which he died peacefully, having been given the assurance by God that Amanda and Belle would be taken care of.

"That day started a journey for me that involved a lot of crying out to God," Amanda said. "I was so shocked, and angry, and hurt. You see, Jaman and I had reached a very difficult spot in our marriage. A lot of people aren't aware of just how much time pastors must devote to caring for the people they serve, and a pastor's family usually gets what is 'left over.' Jaman and I had started down a path leading toward the redemption of our marriage.

"Suddenly I had not only my helpmate, friend, and love taken from me, but also the opportunity to experience a whole and healthy marriage again had been ripped from my arms."

Amada was also left to be a single parent of Belle, then 2½ years old.

"I have been reassured of one thing: God's answer isn't essential to my trust in Him."

"It's been a really painful journey. There have definitely been times I wanted to stay in bed all day. But I couldn't because I have Belle," she said.

"Since that day, I have spent a lot of time crying out to God. I have asked what He saw in me that made Him think I could handle something like this. What is the higher purpose? Where is my life going now?

"I haven't heard a clear answer to my crying out, but I have been reassured of one thing: His answer isn't essential to my trust in Him. The Creator of the universe does not have to meet my demands for full disclosure. In a way, I understand what Job felt like when God responded to him. I have found myself backing away from making demands of God, and instead, truly seeking His face. I had forgotten my first love. I had neglected my relationship with Him. And then, when disaster struck my world, I found myself scrambling."

Amanda had known God's presence in her life was constant. She knew He had never left her. But she also came to realize she had become distant from Him. "It hasn't been until I have welcomed Him back, making it clear I have no idea how to rekindle the romance, that I have sensed His presence and seen His face, in a manner of speaking. That has been my ultimate reward. That has been my answer."

Trying to Process It

As you read Amanda's story, you might feel that knot in your stomach too. *How can this be good? How could God have allowed this?* Yet news reports of the church coming together to carry on Pastor Jaman's legacy of loving others and serving Christ "outside the box" as well as Amanda's personal relationship with Jesus that has been rekindled are just a few of the treasures we can see coming out of this tragedy.

"I can definitely see God's hand and provision in this," Amanda said. "My blessings, amidst the pain, have been my ability to recognize how good God is, how I have never once walked alone, and how His plan for my life will be beautiful.

"I'm not under the impression that it'll be easy from now on, nor that I will never shed another tear. But I have complete confidence that He has already prepared the way before me.

"I am finding it easier to rely on Him these days for all that I am missing by not having my husband. There are still times when I am disappointed, frustrated, sad, or lonely, but I now know that my God has seen my tears, cried them with me, and is walking alongside me as I move forward on His perfect path."

Prior to Jaman's death, Amanda admits "I had completely lost my way."

"I didn't have other godly women who had been in my place, as a pastor's wife, to encourage me. Before Jaman's death, I was holding onto the bitterness and anger that resulted from the hurts we had faced in the ministry. I became so jaded that everyone avoided me. Even through all that, I can look back and see evidence of God loving me. And when Jaman died, and I was so hurt, I saw evidence of God's continued love for me—through the people who loved me, through the cards I received, and through the hugs people gave me. I know that the Creator of the universe was crying and loving me through it all.

"It wasn't until I read the book *When Women Walk Alone*[1] that I realized I hadn't ever walked alone! I then sought God's forgiveness for my anger and bitterness. That, in turn, led to a closer walk with Him. It is amazing what happens when we, as women, give up control. I now rest in complete assurance that God has a beautiful plan for my daughter and me."

Steady Assurances

Amanda has been able to draw comfort and strength from a few conversations she had with Jaman a couple months before he died—conversations that convince her now that God was working back then to give her the peace and assurance that He saw it coming, He was in control, and He would be there for her.

Jaman had told Amanda, about two months before he was shot, that he dreamed that he and Jesus were walking together and Belle was on Jesus' shoulders. Jaman asked Jesus, "Why is Belle on *Your* shoulders? Why isn't she on *mine*? I can carry her. She's my daughter." Jesus' response to Jaman was "*I'm* going to be her protector."

Remembering that conversation with Jaman gave Amanda peace, two months later, when she began to fear the effects of her daughter growing up without a Daddy and protector.

Also, six weeks before Jaman was shot, someone in the congregation had suddenly died. At the memorial service, Jaman had whispered to her, "Amanda, if anything ever happens to me, I want you to grieve me well, and then I want you to move on."

"I took a year to grieve over Jaman, and I believe I grieved him well," Amanda said. "And I am finally able to move on. The pendulum has swung back and forth so often this past year, but now I am fully at peace."

As Amanda recounted her story to me for the first time, it was framed around what God was doing through it all to show His love, provision, and protection to her and little Belle.

> God is still able to do immeasurably more than you expect with the tears you have shed.

Amanda's void was a dependence on God she never even realized she could have. And today, she is beginning to see how God has taken that huge loss in her life and is turning it into a legacy.

"The legacy is that this isn't going to ruin us. We can pick up the pieces. I can look around at the atom bomb destruction and the shock waves of it and I can say, 'You and I can do this, God. And I'm not going to lose sight of who You are. I'm not going to lose track of who You are in my life."

What About You?

I realize you may have experienced the unthinkable in your life as well. A childhood of abuse, a betrayal or broken heart when you were vulnerable, an addiction that took you by surprise, a divorce you never thought would happen, or the loss of someone you dearly loved. Maybe one of your fears suddenly became a reality. Even though I don't know what your unthinkable is, I do know this: Around the corner from the unthinkable exists the God of the Impossible. And He is still able to do immeasurably more than you expect with the tears you have shed. In His love and goodness that you might not understand this side of heaven, He allows the unthinkable so that He can receive insurmountable glory.

When bad things happen to people who aren't living right, we tend to feel a sense of justice. Sometimes a deeper confidence in God results, and we are assured that He really is on the throne and in control of all things.

And yet when bad things happen to people who are loving and serving God? *That* is tough. It is, at times, unthinkable. And sometimes it feels like our good intentions or our life direction and love for God have backfired.

Hannah's Test of Character

When Hannah, whose biblical story we are following, finally pulled herself together, ate, and then slipped away to pray, you'd think at that point there would have been a huge sense of relief. Perhaps that sense of relief and pouring out her heart turned into a peace that began to flood her soul. It would have been nice if it happened that way. Yet Scripture tells us that on the heels of pouring out her heart to God, Hannah was misunderstood and even wrongly accused! I can't help but think this was a character test for Hannah. Would this woman who had just made a vow to God be reverent to this man who was representing God in the midst of his false assumption?

While the false accusation Hannah received is not by any means comparable to what Amanda experienced in losing her husband, it's what happened afterward that helps us realize God is in control even when it looks like we are at the mercy of our circumstances. It shows us that when we're doing the right thing and a misunderstanding or even the unthinkable happens, God is the One who will contend with our adversaries. He expects us to trust Him even when it looks like we have been defeated.

As Hannah prayed to God, her passion was so great that Eli, the high priest, assumed she was drunk. Eli's conclusion is unsettling, as it appears to reflect on the corrupt time during which Hannah was living. Eli's assumption that Hannah was drunk suggests that he was unfamiliar with fervency in prayer, even there in the temple.[2] To give you some background on the condition of the people's hearts during those dark times in biblical history known as "the times of the Judges," Scripture calls Eli's two sons "worthless" and tells us "they did not know the LORD" (1 Samuel 2:12 NASB). We are also told that the sin of those two sons, who were priests, was "very great in the LORD's sight, for they were treating the LORD's offering with contempt" (verse 17). Later, we read these two sons also participated in religious prostitution with the women who served at the temple (verse 22). It was not only a dark, dismal time for Israel, during which the house of God was in great disarray, but a strong contradiction—and a strong irony—for the father of two such immoral and illicit sons to imply that Hannah, a woman of prayer, was acting immorally. For Hannah, the implication was that *she* was a worthless and shameful woman.

Can you imagine praying so intently that you don't care who else is around and, for that, you get accused of being drunk—by a man who is supposed to be religiously astute yet can't even manage the affairs of his own household? How irritating. How hypocritical. How *insulting*.

Yet Hannah responded graciously:

> Not so, my lord...I am a woman who is deeply troubled. I have not been drinking wine or beer; I was pouring out my soul to the LORD. Do not take your servant for a wicked woman; I have been praying here out of my great anguish and grief (1 Samuel 1:15-16).

How could Hannah respond so graciously after being accused so heinously? I'll tell you how—she had just spent some serious time in prayer with God. She knew that God saw her condition and the intentions and sincerity of her heart. She had His peace and knew He had her back.

Experiencing Backfire

How was Amanda able to respond graciously upon hearing the horrific details of her husband's shooting and death and the fact that no one could do anything to revive or resuscitate him? Amanda realized that, even as her universe seemed to be spinning out of control around her, there was a God who was still in control…down to the last detail of how, where, and when her husband died. And she realized that what she learned at the hospital that day had not taken God by surprise.

When something backfires in our life, how we handle it says a great deal about where we have placed our trust.

Have you experienced sudden—or gradual—backfire in your life? Did you marry a man who claimed to be a believer but shortly after the wedding decided he wanted nothing to do with his faith? Have you poured your life into raising your children only to have one of them turn their back on you and go their own rebellious way? Did you commit your new business, project, or future plans to the Lord only to later watch them crumble and fall apart?

How you and I respond to our circumstances tells God and this world where our hope is and on whom we depend. Will you be the kind of woman who gets angry at God for what He allowed? Or will you trust that He is in control and has your back?

How Hannah Handled It

We can gain some valuable insight from Hannah's composure in light of being misunderstood and falsely accused.

1. She was confident that God saw the situation. I find it encouraging that Hannah didn't react negatively to Eli's accusation. Keep in mind that Eli didn't *ask* if Hannah had been drinking, or even if she was drunk. Instead, he had jumped to the conclusion that she *was* drunk. So Hannah had every right, you would think, to correct him. She could have looked at Eli with indignation and come unglued. She could have said, "I've had it. Every year I come here and face a discouraging and extremely stressful situation with my husband's other wife. Then when I finally pull myself together and give it to God in prayer, you, a priest who supposedly represents God, nail me with a judgmental accusation when you don't have a clue as to what's going on here. I don't need this kind of harassment. I'm outta here. And I'm *never* coming back."

Now admit it—you and I might've liked to say something like that if we had been in Hannah's shoes. (It might have made us feel better for at least a moment or two.) But when we are assured that God is aware of every detail of our lives, we can keep our cool knowing He will work everything out according to His plan.

2. She trusted God to clear her name. Although Hannah denied Eli's accusation and told him what she was doing, she also realized she didn't have to make it her job to convince him. Likewise, by being aware that God sees our situation and understands our motives, we can be confident in our integrity and the fact that He will take care of us, reputation and all.

3. She didn't dwell on the offense. Clearly Hannah was the offended party here. Eli should have at least apologized for assuming the worst about her. Surely she could have stormed out of the temple in anger. But she left the matter in God's hands, left graciously, and *still* put her child in Eli's hands a few years later when it was time for her to follow through with her vow to give her child back to the Lord.

It is in our human nature to want retribution. To want an apology. To want to see everything set right. Yet it takes trust and faith to leave retribution in God's hands. Sure enough, God did deal with Eli and his despicable sons in a very severe manner. (You can read about how thoroughly God executed judgment on the house of Eli in 1 Samuel 2:22-36; 3:11-14; 4:10-22.)

When Hannah was gravely misunderstood, she trusted that God knew her heart, would clear her name, and would protect her future. God did just that. And when God executed judgment on the house of Eli, He also anointed Hannah's then-adult son, Samuel, as Israel's foremost priest and prophet.

When Amanda learned that the unthinkable had happened to her husband, she trusted that God knew what He was doing, that He would go before her and Belle, and that He would work everything out. And she's already been seeing God's faithfulness at work. (You will read more about Amanda and Belle in chapter 10.)

How Will *You* Handle It?

Throughout my phone interview with Amanda, now a 31-year-old widowed mom, she could have vented about a beautiful life cut short, about a marriage interrupted, about a daughter who had to grow up without her beloved daddy. She could have expressed great bitterness toward the shooter for taking her husband's life just as they were beginning to realize their dreams together. She could have sworn off service to God or shunned involvement in any church. She could have kissed off her faith altogether because of what it ultimately cost her, her husband, and their family.

But throughout our conversation, her words sounded more like a soft symphony of trust, unwavering faith, and *hope.*

"God definitely orchestrated how Jaman passed from this earth," she said as she recounted the precious details of her husband's last moments before slipping into eternity. "I definitely believe God had been preparing our hearts for this," she added as she recalled the conversations that had taken place between her and Jaman during the weeks prior to his death.

After we finished talking and I hung up the phone, I could not help but wonder if I would be that prepared, that peaceful, that trusting if such a horrible tragedy were to suddenly strike my own family.

At the time I talked with Amanda, my only daughter, Dana, now 21, was on a service project in Kosovo with classmates from her Christian university. She had already been gone for two weeks, and I would not hear from her again until she arrived back in the US in another week. *What if I were to get the devastating news today that my precious daughter is now in God's hands...and that I would never be able to touch hers again this side of heaven?* It was difficult to even fathom.

Tragedy could strike any of us at any time. We hear of it happening to others, and at times we wonder when our day will come. Pain is a part of life because we live in a fallen world. But how we handle what is dealt to us in this life determines our legacy. Will you and I, like Amanda, trust that whatever we go through, God has gone before us and will continue to carry us until our journey on this earth is over?

I want to be like Amanda, who displayed the same attitude as God's righteous servant, Job, who said, "Though He slay me, yet will I trust Him" (Job 13:15 NKJV).

So today I ask myself: Where is my heart when it comes to trusting my Lord with *all* things—both the expected and the unexpected? Where is *yours?*

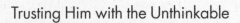

Trusting Him with the Unthinkable

1. What do the following verses tell us to do when we
   begin to worry, doubt or fear? (You may want to write
   your answer below as a reminder to yourself):

   2 Corinthians 10:5—

   Philippians 4:6—

   Philippians 4:8—

   James 1:2-3—

2. What do the following verses say will be the result of
   taking our concerns to God or focusing on His strength?

   Philippians 4:7—

   Philippians 4:13—

   James 1:4—

3. When God didn't answer Amanda's question about *why* her husband had been shot, she replied, "His answer isn't essential to my trust in Him." Would you say you have come to the point where God can withdraw His blessings from you without your trust in Him being affected? Talk this over with God, and write a prayerful response to Him in the space below.

A Prayer of Surrender

Lord God,

You know every detail of my life—all that has happened and what is yet to come. Solidify my trust in You *now* so that when the unthinkable happens, *nothing* comes between the two of us. Help me to be like Your servant Hannah, who held a quiet assurance that You would take care of her situation, protect her reputation, and clear her name, even when she was falsely accused. Help me to be like Your servant Job, who trusted You even when he didn't understand what You were doing in his life. Help me to be like your servant Amanda, who continues to hope in You for the "beautiful" plan You have for her and her daughter, even though You allowed the unthinkable to happen in her life. Thank You that around the corner of the unthinkable is the God of the Impossible, whose love for me is unfathomable.

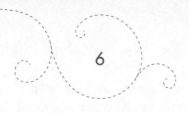

Affirmation

When You're Hanging onto Hope

Eli answered and said, "Go in peace, and
may the God of Israel grant you what you have asked of him."

1 Samuel 1:17

It is natural, when we've been hurt, to no longer want to hope. It's a defense mechanism; it's the way we guard and protect our hearts from further pain.

"It's better not to hope in anything at all than to be disappointed again," we tell ourselves.

Krissy started to slip into that mode of thinking too. But if she had stayed there, she would've lost a tremendous gift—a gift she now has because she chose to hope.

While Krissy was growing up, her father was addicted to pornography, so she saw its ravaging effects on her mother and how she struggled to trust her husband.

"I often wondered why my father would do that, and was just sickened at the thought. Also, just before I met my husband, I had broken off a two-year relationship with a man whom I thought I was going to marry because I discovered he too was addicted to pornography. His addiction destroyed our relationship and my sense of self-worth."

Can you imagine Krissy's devastation when she discovered—two years into her marriage—that her husband struggled with pornography as well?

"He never discussed it with me and hid his problem very well," Krissy said. "I knew he had been exposed to it before we were married, but I just chalked it up to 'that's what single guys do' and expected it to stop once we got married. I had no idea that he was still struggling with pornography until after we had been married for two years, shortly after our daughter was born. I woke up early one morning and he wasn't in bed. I got up to check on him, and he was in front of the television watching a very inappropriate program. He lied and said he had just been flipping through the channels, but I knew better. We talked, and he said he'd stop. Boy was I naïve, but I wanted to believe the best in him. I basically swept it all under the rug and thought, *He will work it out.*

"Every time I caught my husband in this struggle, it broke my heart. He finally came to me one morning—almost eight years into our marriage—and said he was tired of living a lie and wanted to change."

That was the day Krissy had to decide whether she believed God was bigger than an issue that threatened to destroy her marriage.

"It was a few days before Christmas that my husband woke me at 5:30 a.m. He usually left for work around that time and always came in to kiss me good-bye. At first I didn't think much of it. He told me he needed to talk to me. I thought that he was waking me up so that I would know he was leaving and needed me to take care of something while he was at work. It was then that he knelt beside our bed and began sobbing. I sat straight up in bed trying to wake myself up. It was obvious something was bothering him. I was not prepared for the words that came out of his mouth.

"Through his sobbing, he confessed that he'd been secretly looking at pornography on the Internet. I was stunned. I couldn't comprehend what was going on. All I could think was, *No, not again. We can't go down this road again.* I just stayed there and listened while he told me he had been struggling with this again for several months. I didn't know what to say. A flood of emotions filled my mind so fast I couldn't even process them.

"There was no going back to sleep after he left for work. I sat alone in shock. I tried to figure out what I should do. But I *didn't* know what to do. We had dealt with his addiction several times already in our eight-year marriage. The last time we talked, I told him that if it happened again I would leave him. It didn't take long for my shock to turn into anger. *How dare he dump this on me and then leave for work! How could he do this to me again?* I had just reached a point where I trusted him completely. I felt like we were in a good place. I didn't have any suspicions that he had succumbed again. I felt stupid for not seeing it. I felt like I should have known.

"I also felt betrayed. One of the qualities that I loved about my husband when I met him was that he was honest to a fault. What had happened to that honesty? Didn't I still deserve that? I had already been through so much that year with my health and a second miscarriage that had left me very depressed. Hadn't I already dealt with enough heartache? Just as I had managed to pick up the pieces of my life, now this happens?

"Just as I had managed to pick up the pieces of my life, now this happens?"

"A big part of me wanted to pack up his stuff and kick him out. After all, why should *I* leave? I wasn't the one who broke our marriage commitment...yet again. It was then that the anger turned to embarrassment. I couldn't kick him out or leave. Then people would know that something was wrong. I didn't want *anyone* to know. What would people think of him? What would people think of *me*? Would they think it was my fault? Would they think that I didn't make myself available to him enough? I thought about our children. How would I explain why mom and dad weren't living in the same house? I couldn't do that to them. I then decided that I would just sleep on the floor beside our bed. I didn't want my husband to accidentally touch me during the night. The thought of him touching me made me sick to my stomach."

As the questions continued to go through Krissy's mind, the pain she had overcome from dealing with her husband's previous struggles came flooding back. She kept asking herself, *What have I done to deserve this?*

A Change of Heart

"It was during this pity party I was throwing for myself that I came to realize an important point. This was *his* problem, not mine. It had nothing to do with me. It wasn't because I wasn't there for him. It wasn't because he didn't find me attractive anymore. It wasn't that we were drifting apart. It wasn't that he didn't love me. I was suddenly filled with an overwhelming sense of compassion for him. I thought about how much guilt he had been carrying around knowing that he was deceiving me all that time. I thought about the fear he must have been feeling as he broke my heart again. I wondered if he was worried about how I was going to react when he got home that evening. I knew how much he loved me and our children. I knew he never meant to hurt me. I wanted to be angry, but couldn't. I actually felt *peace*.

"That evening when he got home, he sat next to me on the couch. I didn't say much. I was still trying to process how I was feeling and struggling with the fact that I wasn't as angry as I felt I should be. As we began talking, he told me he really wanted to be free from the bondage that this addiction had on his life. He promised to do anything it took for me to trust him again. He apologized that he had allowed this to creep back into his life and our marriage. A part of me wanted to remind him that I had heard all this before and here we were again, but I didn't say that. I just sat and listened, which was a significant accomplishment for me because I had a tendency to just spew out my thoughts when I was upset.

"He told me that once he arrived at work that day he had called one of our pastors who had previously counseled him on this issue. Our pastor gave him the phone number of a Christian counselor. Then my husband also called our family doctor and asked for a recommendation for a Christian counselor. He then talked to the benefits coordinator at work about insurance coverage for a therapist. After that he made several calls and found a male Christian therapist and made an appointment. I was impressed that he had done all of that in one day and all on his own. I was proud of him.

"As the night went on we sat in silence on the couch together and watched television. I couldn't remember the last time we had even sat next to each other on the same couch or even taken time to just talk. The busyness of our lives had taken its toll in recent years. We both worked full time, and he had gone back to school. There was homework to be done, ministry obligations, dance practices, and children to feed and bathe. Somehow, in that silence next to him on the couch, I felt a connection to him again. I felt an overwhelming urge to kiss him. As I leaned over and kissed him, his eyes filled with tears. I began to cry as I told him I still loved him and I wanted to see him fix this because I didn't want to live the rest of our lives going back and forth with these feelings. By the end of the night we found ourselves entangled in each other's arms in the act of marriage. I didn't understand how I could go from being so hurt and angry at him to being intimate with him so quickly. It just felt right.

"After that night I was still heartbroken. I had days during which I could accept his struggles and the fact he was working to resolve them. Other days, I was bitter and furious. I just couldn't drop it and, at times, I brought it up unnecessarily just to hurt him. I wish his difficulties with pornography had truly come to an end, but the truth is he still struggles and I've come to realize that he always will. But the fact that he's fighting the problem and has given it to God means we can get through it. We both had to realize that we can't fight this battle on our own.

"Before I surrendered it to God, I would often cry out to Him in anger. I was mad and felt punished. I asked what I had done to deserve this. I asked God, in bitterness, to make my husband literally sick if he even thought about pornography or sought it out. After the anger and bitterness, though, I became broken. It seemed like I found myself crying out the most through Christian songs. I would hear songs about God being present in the midst of the storms and songs about following Him in the midst of trials. I downloaded songs like these on my iPod and listened to them constantly. While listening, tears would pour down my face and I would cry out to God with all my voice. When I felt I had nothing more to give, I felt His peace and comfort. I didn't feel alone. I just sensed that everything was under control. It was in *His* control, not mine.

"So I filled my mind with Scripture through these songs that I listened to while driving to work, while at work, while driving home, and at night before bed just so I could rest assured that God was in control. He was working on me through it all. Oh, how I wish I had listened sooner."

Holding onto Hope

Krissy was able to replace her resentment and fear with hope when she realized her hope is not in her husband. Her hope is not in a 3-step plan or a 12-step program. Her hope is not in anything this world has to offer. Rather, her hope is in God, who can, at any time, completely remove this obstacle from their lives…or teach them to walk alongside Him as they depend on Him for daily strength.

Krissy finds personal encouragement and hope for her marriage in a passage of Scripture that assures her that not only is God working this situation for good in their lives, causing them both to be more dependent on Him, but He is transforming both of them into His image:

> We know that God causes all things to work together
> for good to those who love God, to those who are called
> according to His purpose. For those whom He foreknew,
> He also predestined to become conformed to the image
> of His Son (Romans 8:28-29 NASB).

Can God work even through a temptation, a struggle, an issue that has torn so many marriages apart? Yes. And, if nothing else, through Krissy's brokenness and her dependence on God—as well as her acknowledgment that He is in control of everything and she is not—she is becoming more like Christ.

"It might sound strange, but the biggest blessing that has come out of this situation is the realization that I'm a sinner. I've been raised in church all my life. I've heard the stories of those who have wandered and gotten into 'the things of the world.' That was never me. I didn't have one of those stories. I was the one who stayed in church, worked in the nursery, served on the worship team, and so on. *I wasn't one of those people who strayed*, I thought. *I wasn't like my husband, who was living in sin,* I told myself.

"I held a grudge for a long time, but one day during a worship service at church we began to sing about the blood of Jesus, and it hit me that I was a sinner and the same blood that had washed my sins away was there for my husband too. Talk about humbling! I cried like a baby. If God could forgive me for letting Him down time and time again, then I could forgive my husband too. That's when things really started to change. I was expecting my husband to 'change his ways or else,' but *I* had to change too. It was after my heart was softened that I could turn the years of pain, suffering, misery, and anger into forgiveness. When the forgiveness on my part started, my husband and I became closer than ever before."

How is Krissy able to maintain hope in spite of fears and doubts that could invade her mind at any time? She has taken the advice

of the song writer in Psalm 42:11—someone else who had also battled feelings of despair:

> Why, my soul, are you downcast?
>   Why so disturbed within me?
> *Put your hope in God,*
>   for I will yet praise him,
>   my Savior and my God.

Even though Krissy had been frustrated by her husband's fre-
quent struggles with pornography and even though she knew this
addiction seemed to have great power over men, she realized God
is bigger than all of that. And He is a God in whom she can put her
trust *and* hope. Though others may let her down, she knows that
God Himself is incapable of disappointing her.

Hannah's Hope

Hannah also reached a point where she had to decide whether
she would look back at her past pain and harbor ill feelings, remain
in doubt, and be miserable all her days—or free herself from cynicism and start hoping in the God who was in control. I'm so glad
she let go of her fear of being disappointed and decided to trust the
all-knowing, all-hearing, all-seeing God.

According to the scriptural account of Hannah's story, when Eli
learned that Hannah had not been drunk but instead had been
praying fervently, he didn't ask what she had been praying about. He
simply said, "Go in peace, and may the God of Israel grant you what
you have asked of him" (1 Samuel 1:17). Eli didn't say "May God
give you a child." In fact, Eli didn't even know what Hannah had
prayed for. Perhaps he was being gentlemanly—or apologetic—by
saying, "I hope God gives you what you were asking for." But Hannah knew God had heard her, and perhaps she considered Eli's comment a confirmation that God was already working on her request.

First Samuel 1:18-20 tells us Hannah's response—and God's:

She said, "May your servant find favor in your eyes." Then she went her way and ate something, and her face was no longer downcast.

Early the next morning they arose and worshiped before the LORD and then went back to their home at Ramah. Elkanah made love to his wife Hannah, *and the LORD remembered her.* So in the course of time Hannah became pregnant and gave birth to a son. She named him Samuel, saying, "Because I asked the LORD for him."

Hannah left that place a different woman, a new woman— a woman of hope who would wait on God for her request to be realized.

It's important to note that Hannah maintained hope in God even though she didn't see an immediate fulfillment of her desire. I believe Hannah was hopeful because

- she knew God had heard her prayer.
- she held nothing back and trusted God would honor that.
- she had made a vow she knew God would take seriously.

I find it interesting that after Eli told Hannah, "May the Lord grant your request" she didn't brush it off as wishful thinking. She didn't feel the need to give Eli more information that would put him in his place for even suggesting such a thing. She didn't respond as you or I might have considering all that had happened that day: "Thank you, Mr. Eli. It would be nice if God did grant my request. But you see, I was asking for the same thing I've requested of God for several years—I was asking for a baby. And being that I'm barren, it's difficult for me to get my hopes up about it anymore. So it would be best if *you* didn't get my hopes up. In fact, why don't you just pray that I have peace from this point onward?"

A response like that would've implied that Hannah never

expected God to come through with her request. Instead of having to have the last say in the situation, Hannah responded graciously by saying "Sir, thank you for being so kind to me" (CEV).

Hannah must have realized she had done her part—by making her request—and she could do no more. She prayed in faith, expecting God to come through. And apparently she knew the rest was up to Him.

That is sometimes where you and I go wrong. We believe what we are praying for is up to us every step of the way, or we give up—perhaps right before God was getting ready to grant our request.

Our Hesitancy to Hope

I remember feeling, during my college years, that it was better not to hope in anything at all than to be disappointed again. I had gone through a couple of months during which I felt that every relationship I had been in had disappointed me, every project I attempted failed, every hope I had was dashed. (Looking back now, I'm sure it wasn't a case of *every*, but it sure felt like it at the time.) I didn't realize how cynical I had become until a friend finally asked me why I always expected the worst. I found myself saying, "It's better not to hope at all than to hope and be disappointed." Wow! Had I really become that pessimistic?

As I grew in my walk with God, I began to realize how very insulting it is to God to be a person who expects the worst. Although it was unintentional, I was saying to myself—and everyone around me—"I don't believe God has power over this, and I don't expect Him to surprise me with what He can do." Again, it's not necessarily what I was *verbalizing,* or even consciously thinking, but that must have been the impression I was giving to others.

Hebrews 11:1 says, "Now faith is the assurance of things hoped for, the conviction of things not seen" (NASB). And verse 6 adds, "without faith it is impossible to please [God]." Was my cynicism pleasing to God? Absolutely not! Even people who don't know God can be optimistic—hoping in fate or luck or their own ability. How sad that I was a child of God and I wasn't giving Him credit for being the kind of Father who loves to give good gifts to His children (Matthew 7:11).

At first I didn't see my cynicism as a lack of faith and an insult to the power and ability of God. Rather, I thought I was protecting my heart and shielding myself from further disappointment. And yet Scripture calls God the "God of hope" who fills us with all joy and peace as we trust in Him, so that we "may overflow with hope by the power of the Holy Spirit" (Romans 15:13). Hope is a defining characteristic of those who are children of God. Think about that. Having hope—and being able to hang onto His promises—is not only a characteristic of one who is His. It is *evidence* that we are His.

Practicing Hope

Let's look now at how *you* can be a woman who practices hope even when there might not be anything in your situation that looks hopeful.

Hope in His Word

Did you know that God cannot contradict His Word? While He has guidelines in Scripture that are not necessarily promises, there are passages that contain promises that hold true as we obey Him. For example, 2 Corinthians 1:20 tells us, "For all the promises of God in Him are Yes, and in Him Amen, to the glory of God through us" (NKJV).

> The more you trust God, the less you will doubt, worry, fear, or give up.

Hope in His Character

God also cannot contradict Himself. So when He says in His Word that He causes all things to work together for good to those who are called according to His purpose,[1] He will do just that. He will take care of what you put into His hands. The more you get to know Him, the more you will trust Him. The more you trust Him, the less you will doubt, worry, fear, or give up. Just as 1 Corinthians 13:7 tells us how to love others, it also tells us how to love God. Love (for God) "bears all things, believes all things, *hopes all things*, endures all things" (NKJV). You might be in the "bears all things" or the "endures all things" stage right now. But make sure you are believing and hoping too. Doesn't God deserve to hear you lovingly whisper, "Lord, I believe in You and Your timing. And I know You will come through for me in a way that You see is best"?

Hope in His Timing

This is key, as we will see in the next chapter. God knows exactly when you are ready to receive the desire of your heart, and He will not act a moment too soon or a moment too late when it comes to doing what is eternally best for you. When you are in the long haul of waiting and you aren't getting a *yes*, will you trust that what you might think is a *no* might really be His *wait*? He knows best. And therefore His timing is always perfect.

Live with Expectancy

For years, I have found hope in this passage of Scripture:

> This is the confidence which we have before Him, that, if we ask anything according to His will, He hears us. And if we know that He hears us *in* whatever we ask, we know that we have the requests which we have asked from Him (1 John 5:14-15 NASB).

This verse tells me that (1) I can be confident when I pray in this way; (2) when I ask according to God's will, He will hear my request; and (3) if I know He hears me in whatever I ask, I know I have received what I've asked of Him.

As you and I spend time with God in prayer and in His Word, we will get to know His heart, and eventually we will begin to ask for what He would ask for, which is what it means to ask "according to His will."

As we do that, we can begin to live in what Oswald Chambers calls a *constant state of expectancy*: "Keep your life so constantly in touch with God that His surprising power can break through at any point. Live in a constant state of expectancy, and leave room for God to come in as He decides."[2]

How do you and I go from fearing the worst to expecting the best on a daily basis? By realizing the circumstances of your life haven't happened by chance. By realizing there is One who oversees everything that happens in your life and loves you more than you can fathom. By trusting that if He's waiting, or allowing hardships, or declining to answer you just now, He has a reason. Most likely, He is preparing you for the day you will receive what He has for you.

He Will Remember

After Hannah poured her heart out to God in prayer, surrendered what she was asking for, and believed that God had heard her, Hannah chose to expect the best. And we are told what happened after "her face was no longer downcast."

> Early the next morning they arose and worshiped before the Lord and then went back to their home at Ramah. Elkanah lay with Hannah his wife, and *the Lord remembered her* (verse 19).

Now those are four words I've been waiting this whole book to talk about: "the Lord remembered her." Stick with me. That's where we're going next.

In the meantime, keep hoping in Him, my friend. And He *will* remember *you*.

Maintaining Hope in the Midst of Heartache

1. How can you apply 1 Corinthians 13:7 and bear all things, believe all things, hope all things, and endure all things in your present situation?

2. What would it take for you to live in a *constant state of expectancy*, waiting for God to show up and intervene at any time?

3. What promises from Scripture are you clinging to right now? (If you don't have or know of any, see Appendix B on pages 195-207 for some to claim and cling to as your own.)

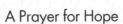

A Prayer for Hope

Lord Jesus,

I want to stand apart as Your child by being a person who looks to You for the impossible, the improbable, and the unbelievable. I know You want that of me too. So please fill me with all joy and peace as I trust in You so that I may overflow with hope by the power of the Holy Spirit (Romans 15:13). Help me to live in a constant state of expectancy, always ready to let you work in my life however You want. Finally, help me to hope in *You*, not merely in what I want You to *do*.

7

The Arrival

When Your Prayers Are Finally Answered

The LORD remembered her plea, *and in
due time* she gave birth to a son.

1 SAMUEL 1:19-20 (NLT)

Christina Lee knows what it's like to wait on the Lord for the desire of her heart…and to continue to hope in spite of disappointment.

She and her husband, Ben, waited more than a decade for God to "remember their plea" and grant their heart's desire for a child. The waiting wasn't easy. At times, it was even painful. But they will both tell you it was worth the wait. God had a work He wanted to accomplish "in due time." And He had a gift He was preparing for her and her husband that was beyond their expectations.

"I have often felt like Hannah," Christina said. "Hannah received her blessing in the midst of sorrow. I too have received that."

Rather than experiencing a nine-month pregnancy, Christina and her husband experienced a 15-year wait that involved a lot of praying and trusting the God who overcomes all odds.

Not only did they pray for a child all through those years, but family, friends, and many others who have moved in and out of their sphere of ministry have prayed for them to become parents as well. While the waiting was difficult, Christina never lost hope.

Christina has long quoted verses of Scripture as her promises from God that she would one day have children. She put her hope in verses such as Psalm 127:3, which says, "Children are a gift from the Lord; they are a reward from him" (NLT).

"I believe that in the Bible there are many promises for us. And I believe children are one of those promises," Christina said. "But after many years of trying and seeing no results, we began to cry out to the Lord."

During those years, while God didn't appear to be delivering on His promise for a baby, He continued to confirm to Christina, over and over again, that He had not forgotten her.

"He has either given me a scripture at just the right time about having children, or He has reaffirmed His promise to me with people praying for me about having children. There were even some people praying for me who did not know my situation."

Christina recalls the day a woman prayed for her very specifically that her desire for children would be granted. "At that point in my life I was feeling pretty low about not having children. Before this woman prayed for me, I asked the Lord in simple, childlike faith to give me assurance that He had not forgotten me. I was so done with the disappointment month after month, and I needed Him to uplift me. This woman did not know me, for this was the first time I had met her. As she laid her hands on me, the first thing she said to me was, 'Your children will rise up and call you blessed' from Proverbs 31:28. In response, I wept before the Lord. Things like this have happened to me over and over. So I knew I was bound to have children."

And, just as in Hannah's case, the day came when God "remembered" Christina and "in the course of due time" granted her request for a child. But it wasn't in the way that she and her husband had expected, or even dreamed. It was far better.

Gradual Confirmation

A family in Ben and Christina's church had a niece, a methamphetamine addict named "Jenny" whose boyfriend was an alleged drug dealer. Jenny had experienced several pregnancies and abortions and birthed several children in spite of her addiction. Her "Aunt Jan" rescued three of those children and adopted them into her home. At this time the children were ages 3, 5, and 6. Around January of 2010, Jenny was pregnant again. This time she told her aunt and uncle that she was either going to jail or going to abort the baby. Jan and her husband, Ken, are both Christians and they didn't want to see Jenny's baby aborted. They prayed for her to go to jail instead so the baby would be protected. Christina said that when Jenny was pregnant with her other three children she had continued to use drugs. But this time, because Jenny ended up going to jail early in the pregnancy, the baby was able to develop within her drug-free.

"Praise God, the Lord was watching over him even in the womb," Christina said.

Jenny stayed in jail until she was 8½ months pregnant. She then moved in with her Aunt Jan and Uncle Ken until she delivered the baby. During the entire pregnancy, Ben and Christina had not even thought about adopting Jenny's baby. They were, instead, trying to help her get into a Christian women's home. But Jenny didn't want to be away from her boyfriend, who was still using drugs. A little while later, she delivered a perfectly healthy baby boy and brought him to church with her aunt and uncle.

"He was beautiful, and she allowed me to hold him," Christina said. "As soon as I held him, I sensed the Lord saying, 'This child is yours.' Now this was overwhelming. But I told Aunt Jan that if Jenny happened to return to drugs, she could call us, and we would take the baby.

"What I didn't know is that Jenny's Uncle Ken, a longtime friend of ours, knew from the beginning that the baby was to be ours. I guess when Jenny found out she was pregnant, Ken was praying about the whole matter. The whole time, he didn't say anything to us. On the night that Jenny brought her newborn son to church, Jan called and said she knew Jenny was back on drugs. She wondered if we would take the baby. Without even pausing to think about it, we both said, 'Yes!' This was the beginning of our journey.

"Of course I wanted to make sure this was from the Lord. (I had heard horror stories of people trying to adopt a child only for the birth parents to take the child back. I feared that might happen to me.) I was talking to my mom about my concern, and she said, 'Let's pray and ask the Lord to show us if this baby is for us.' As we prayed, the words *spirit of adoption* came to mind. As we kept praying, the reference *Romans 8* surfaced in my thoughts as well."

Christina knew that in Scripture, the phrase "spirit of adoption" refers to those who are adopted into God's family through faith in Christ. But she applied that verse to her personal situation and believed God was talking to her, personally, through His Word.

"At that moment the Word of God gave me peace..."

"At that time, I wasn't sure if that phrase was in Romans 8. I asked my mom if 'spirit of adoption' was in Romans 8 and she wasn't sure either. So we looked it up, and sure enough, those words appear in Romans 8:15. I sensed then that the Lord was saying that the 'spirit of adoption' was on Gabriel. At that moment the Word of God gave me peace, and I knew no matter what happened, Gabriel was ours."

Christina had further confirmation when she went home and spoke to her husband that evening.

"When I got home and told Ben about the phrase 'spirit of adoption' during our prayer, he said, 'That's funny because yesterday I was praying about Gabriel and I thought of Romans 8:15 and what it says about the spirit of adoption. I asked the Lord to confirm His Word by showing you.'"

Christina said even though she and Ben knew that Gabriel would be theirs, there was opposition, and on many occasions they went back to God in prayer and pleading.

"Within the week of Jan telling us Jenny was on drugs, Jenny ran from Child Protection Services with Gabriel," Christina said. "CPS had come to her door and she fled in the car with him. When I heard this news, I went into my prayer closet and prayed for Jenny to be found. I prayed with great fervency. The next day, Jenny gave Gabriel to her boyfriend, who didn't want CPS knocking on his door, so he dropped off Gabriel at the police station. We got a phone call that night from Jan saying Gabriel was with an emergency foster mom."

Ben and Christina immediately started attending foster care classes to become certified as foster parents so they could take care of Gabriel in their home. Many people warned them that obtaining legal custody of Gabriel and then being able to adopt him would be a long, drawn-out process.

Gabriel's Arrival

Shortly after Ben and Christina started taking foster care classes, Jenny agreed to make them the legal guardians of Gabriel. Just seven weeks after they started the process of obtaining custody of Gabriel, Christina got an unexpected visit in early December while on the job at a preschool. Having been told by CPS that it was going to be a long, slow process before they received Gabriel, she didn't expect that she would hear any news anytime soon.

"I was closing down my school when suddenly Ben came through the door holding Gabriel in a little Santa's Helper outfit. We finally got him, praise Jesus! I knew that no matter what happened, he was ours forever. The birth parents saw Gabriel a few times through CPS, but each time that happened I knew he was going to continue to stay with us. We had favor with the parent aid, who told us exactly what was happening at every stage in the process. Our case manager was a blessing to us and for us.

"God also gave Ben favor with the court system—as it turned out, we went to court at the exact same place where Ben worked. All the judges knew and loved Ben. In the summer of 2012 we got word during our vacation that both of the birth parents' rights were severed and we could file for adoption. We were warned it would take a long time for this to be approved. Even our lawyer said it was impossible to have him adopted by the end of that year, but we maintained hope. Ben went to one of the judges he knew and asked if she could help out. She moved up our case on the court calendar and we ended up adopting Gabriel exactly one year from the day we received legal custody of him.

"Everyone was amazed that it happened so quickly, and we gave glory to the Lord and said it was all Him. This is our wonderful God story. It is a story filled with grace, love, and hope in our Lord Jesus Christ and what He does for His children. We are truly blessed and not a day goes by when we don't thank the Lord for His goodness and mercy toward us. He truly has given us the desire of our hearts. We truly believe Gabriel was made for us."

God's timing is often different than ours. Yet it is always perfect.

I had the privilege of meeting little Gabriel and have seen him on a few occasions since. And let me tell you, this little boy, now nearly four years old, looks so much like his adoptive parents it's uncanny. "Even his behavior resembles the two of us and he is always joyful," Christina said.

"I give God all the glory for what He has done, and I love sharing my story so people can be encouraged and know that God *is* faithful to His children."

God's Perfect Timing

Now that Christina's hope is realized through her son Gabriel, she is able to see clearly that God knew exactly what He was doing during those long years of waiting. He was divinely orchestrating her and Ben's every move so they would be in just the right place, at just the right time, to become Gabriel's new parents.

"In the Process of Time"

In Hannah's story, there is a phrase that is worth careful consideration when it comes to the requests we lay before God. In 1 Samuel 1:19-20 we read that God saw Hannah's tears, He "remembered" her request, and "*in the process of time*...Hannah conceived and bore a son, and called his name Samuel, saying, 'Because I have asked for him from the LORD'" (NKJV).

God's timing is often different than ours. Yet it is always perfect. Hannah had waited a long time before God granted her a child—Scripture says that "in the process of time" she conceived. What was God doing during that "process of time"? It is very likely that He was

- developing Hannah's ability to trust Him
- developing in her such a strong desire for a child that she would offer him back to the Lord
- developing her character so she would be the kind of mom He wanted her to be
- arranging the point in history at which time Samuel would arrive at Eli's house and then grow to become Israel's prophet and priest

God had quite a few things He wanted to accomplish "in the process of time" when it came to Hannah, her anticipated son Samuel, and the nation of Israel. And God had some things He wanted to accomplish "in the process of time" with Ben and Christina too. He apparently wanted to

- nuture Ben and Christina toward complete dependency on Him so they would consult with Him at every turn
- prepare a baby for them at just the right time
- prepare them for the faith it would take to stick through

the process of becoming foster care parents and adoptive
parents

- bring them closer together through His assurances to
them of His plan

- strengthen their faith to never doubt how He works in
the lives of those who trust Him and His Word

Could God be waiting on *your* request because there are different works He wants to accomplish "in the process of time"? And
could those works include things He is doing in *you* to strengthen
your faith and make you more dependent on Him?

When God Hasn't Delivered

By now you might be thinking, *Well, it's great that Hannah and
Christina finally got what they hoped and prayed for. But what about
me? Where is my big break? When is God going to bless me with my
request?* Maybe you're even wondering, *What if God's process of time
means never?* If that is the case, I have some encouragement for you:
Sometimes God hasn't delivered on your request because He's waiting to give you what you haven't yet asked for.

Again, if God is withholding something from you, He knows,
in His infinite wisdom, that not granting your request right now or
not granting it in the way you have asked is far better for you. You
might never understand that this side of heaven. But if He is withholding anything from you, at least from your human perspective,
it's either because it's not good for you, or it's not quite the right time,
or because He has a far better *yes* in store for you. He is, most likely,
waiting to bless you with what *He* wants you to desire.

You see, originally Hannah just wanted a child. But God didn't
want to give her *just a child*. When God granted Hannah's request,
it wasn't so she would be a happy homemaker and feel she had all
she needed. It wasn't so she could get even with Peninnah, who had
many children. God had a plan—and a divine destiny—for this
child Hannah would bear and give back to Him. God had a prophet

to raise up, a king to anoint, a nation to restore—and He was going to do those divinely ordained things through Hannah's child, Samuel. Hannah had no idea what God had in store when she offered to give her much-longed-for son back to God in service. Again, she just wanted a baby. But God wanted to change history. Hannah just wanted to be a mom. God wanted to give her a legacy. So what Hannah originally perceived as a *no* answer from God was really God saying, "Not yet. I want to give you something far greater than you have thought to ask for."

When Hannah finally said, "If you give me a male child, I will give him back to you," she was in the place where she was surrendered to God's will. She was ready for the child to be used in the way God desired. Again, if Samuel hadn't been raised in the house of Eli, he probably wouldn't have grown to become a mighty prophet. God had it all planned out, but Hannah had to align her life with His plan—and surrender to God's purposes and desires rather than seek her own.

Let's apply this to your situation. If you are wanting something very badly, would you consider wanting it so that *God* can be glorified, so that *He* can change history with it, so that *He* can build into you a legacy with it…or without it? When you are willing to accept God's answer, whether it is *yes* or *no* or *wait*, then you will have put yourself into the place where God can use you, no matter what His answer.

What's in the Garage?

I love a story Dr. Henry Blackaby tells in the book *Experiencing God*.

He decided that his eldest son, Richard, was old enough to have a bicycle for his sixth birthday. So he looked all around for a bicycle. He found a blue Schwinn bicycle, bought it, and hid it in the garage. Then his task was to convince Richard that he needed a blue Schwinn bike.

Blackaby says, "For the next little while, we began to work with

Richard. Richard decided that what he really wanted for his birthday was a blue Schwinn bike. Do you know what Richard got? Well, the bike was already in the garage. I just had to convince him to ask for it. He asked for it and he got it!"

Blackaby says when we pray, "The Holy Spirit knows what God has 'in the garage.' It is already there. The Holy Spirit's task is to get you to want it—to get you to ask for it. What will happen when you ask for things God already wants to give or do? You will always receive it. Why? Because you have asked according to the will of God. When God answers our prayer, He gets the glory and your faith is increased."[1] Philippians 2:13 tells us, "It is God who works in you to will and to act in order to fulfill his good purpose." In the New Living Translation, that verse says: "God is working in you, giving you the desire and the power to do what pleases him."

Ben and Christina could have just naturally had a desire for children, as many married couples do. But at the right time, God put in them a specific desire for little Gabriel. God knew—before they married, before they even met, before the very beginning of time—which little boy would be hand-picked for them. He knew exactly who little Gabriel's parents needed to be. And He began to work on Ben and Christina "in the process of time" to get them to ask Him specifically for little Gabriel.

What might God have "in the garage" for you? You might think it's something tangible like a baby, or a husband, or a more successful career, or a fulfilled dream. But God might have something for you that is far more valuable—something that you haven't even thought to ask for. It could be more along the lines of a more compassionate heart for others, a ministry to other women who have experienced similar hurts, or possibly even a position in which you will be able to influence *hundreds* of people instead of a handful—or *thousands* of children rather than just one or two.

Do you want to receive what God has "in the garage" for you? Ask Him to examine your heart, to align your desires with His, to make you want what He wants for you. As Psalm 37:4 says, "Delight yourself in the LORD, and He will give you the desires of your heart." Another way you could read that verse is, "Delight yourself in the Lord, and He will place in Your heart *His* desires...and then He will delight in granting them."

God's Intentions for Us

When Michele (from chapter 4) asked to be restored, she asked that God would receive the glory from her life. And God receives the glory every time Michele opens her mouth and tells people of the pit she was in and how God pulled her out of it. He is able to receive glory from her life not just someday when "everything is worked out," but every day that she surrenders her life to Him and says to Him and others, "I'm not there yet, but God is doing a work in me."

When Gayla asked for God's divine healing in the lives of the three women she ultimately lost, God knew He could do more in her life and in the lives of those she ministers to by keeping her dependent upon Him during those losses and by bringing her through the brokenness. Today Gayla is able to minister to others even more effectively because of the valleys of darkness and loss she has walked through. She can comfort others with the comfort she has received from God.

Oh how God wants to bless us! If only we would start asking for what *He* wants to give us.

Listen for Him

As we become tuned in to what God wants for us, we may come to recognize that He *is* answering—and speaking with us—far more than we had realized.

For Ben and Christina to have all those assurances about baby Gabriel, for them to each get confirmation on even the same day through their various circumstances, is a testimony to their years of listening to God, searching His Word, being in His presence through prayer, and showing Him that they would await His answer "in the process of time."

God often does not give us what we want the moment we ask for it because He is interested in the relationship. The more we sit before Him, wait on Him, and keep coming back, the more we get to know Him, recognize His voice, and become familiar with His heart. God wants you to keep coming back to Him because He loves you. And when He can trust You to wait for Him, to go when he says "Go" and to wait when He says "Wait," then that may be when He can trust you with what you have requested.

God is far more concerned with what you need than what you want. And He knows exactly what He wants to do with whatever you ask Him for. He had a plan for Hannah's life (and the life of her son) and she had yet to discover it. He had a plan for Ben and Christina, and they had yet to discover it. And He has a plan for *your* life too. Will you trust Him with His plan? And will you start listening for what His desires are for your life?

Remember, His timing is perfect. Be willing to wait and see what He does—"in the process of time."

Trusting His Process of Time

Read Ecclesiastes 3:1-8, then take time to reflect on what God has asked you to wait for. Of the things that God eventually gave you, what have been the benefits of His timing? Of the things He has not yet given you, what might He want to do in you—or someone else—*in the process of time?*

A Prayer He Wants to Answer

God,

Your very greatest, most loving gift to us is something that cost you dearly. You gave us Your Son—God in the flesh—so we could see a demonstration of how much You loved us and wanted us to put our faith in You.

So as I come to You with my heart set on what I want, help me to remember that Your timing and Your preferred way of doing things is perfect. Help me not to second-guess You, God, by assuming my ways are better. Your ways are higher than my ways, and Your thoughts so much better than mine (Isaiah 55:8-9).

Thank You for all Your good and perfect gifts, and thank You as well for what You have chosen to not yet give me. Help me to understand that Your "wait" is because You have some work You want to first accomplish in me or others who may be a part of Your answer. Accomplish in me what You desire—in the process of time.

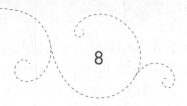

8

The Ultimate Sacrifice

When You Give It Back to God

I prayed for this child, and the LORD has granted me
what I asked of him. So now I give him to the LORD...

1 SAMUEL 1:27-28

At 36 years of age, Dawn was facing widowhood far earlier than she
ever imagined.

"How can this be good, God?" she asked as she waited to hear
the update on her husband's condition after he suffered a heart
aneurism.

"The whole time I was in the hospital ER waiting for the doctor to come out, I was praying that God would save my husband,"
Dawn said. "However, that wasn't God's plan. God's answer to me
was 'No. Trust Me.'"

Trusting God when He seems to ask the impossible is one of
the most difficult things He asks of us. Step inside of Dawn's pain
for a moment as she describes to you what she was feeling as God
was asking her to surrender to *His* plan, which meant the loss of her
husband:

"I was very angry at God. After all, He is all-knowing, all-seeing,
and could have prevented my husband's death, right? But He proved
that He was big enough to handle me and my anger. I learned that
I didn't have to drive myself crazy over my cycles of anger and guilt.
It's okay to be angry and not sin (Ephesians 4:26). I can tell God

how I feel. I also learned just how tiny a mustard seed is. God said if we have faith even the size of a mustard seed, we can do just about anything.[1] I relied on that truth during my grief journey.

"Later, as the pain of grief and loneliness set in, I began to crave a new relationship. God's answer to me was 'Wait. Trust Me.' I covered my ears to His voice and allowed my desperation to push me toward a relationship that wasn't good for me. I should have allowed God to direct my path, but I didn't. God's answer in that relationship was once again 'No. Trust Me.' It took me a while, but when I finally decided to trust God with my future, I felt peace for the first time since York died. I was able to reach outside myself and begin helping others. I volunteered as a helper at my church's clothing closet and food pantry. I met new friends. Then in 2009 I met a friend at church who later became my husband. He's my greatest supporter and respects my past."

Dawn's story doesn't mean that every widow will travel the same path and eventually remarry. It ultimately depends on what God sees as best for a woman who agrees to trust Him—even when He's saying, "Wait"; even when He's saying, "No."

"A grief journey is long and difficult, perhaps one of the most difficult journeys you face in life," Dawn said. "You don't wake up one morning and suddenly decide everything has returned to perfect again. It hasn't. You're a work in progress. You make mistakes. You feel sorry for yourself. You grieve, but you know God is with you.

"God knows what He is doing."

"My biggest blessing was discovering that the Lord has promised to care for me. He said in His Word He would look after the widows and orphans (Psalm 146:9). I clung to that promise. He also brought people into my life that I never would have met had I not gone through this journey. My parents keep reminding me that when we go through trials we can be assured that God will not waste the experience. We can use our trials as opportunities to reach out to others.

"Another blessing has been meeting my current husband, Alex, and adopting our beautiful eight-year-old daughter. God has placed a yearning in our hearts to reach out to children in foster care. We're getting ready to open our home again. These are blessings I could not have experienced if the Lord had not allowed me to become a widow. Yes, I wish things could have been different. Would I go back and change what had happened if I could? No. God knows what He's doing."

Did you catch Dawn's last statement? It was her declaration of faith during the ultimate test. That is a key point for us to comprehend when it comes to trusting God with whatever He asks of us: *God knows what He is doing.*

Faith and Sacrifice

The Bible contains story after story of real-life people who had to decide whether or not they would exercise faith and trust that God knew what He was doing, even in the face of great personal sacrifice or incredible odds. Throughout those stories we come to see that faith and an unswerving trust in God are characteristic of those who are His.

Scripture defines faith as "the assurance of things hoped for, the conviction of things not seen" (Hebrews 11:1 NASB). And that kind of faith—the kind that trusts God's promises—is what He still demands of us today as evidence that we are His, that we love Him, and that we believe Scripture's declarations that He is a good and loving God who wants only the best for His children.

In the Old Testament we read of Abraham, whom God told to take his beloved son, Isaac, up Mount Moriah and offer him there as a burnt sacrifice in order to prove his obedience to God. *How can this be good, God?* Abraham may have thought. *I've waited twenty-five years for You to fulfill Your promise of giving me a son in my old age, and now, when he's still a boy, You want me to give him back to You by burning him as a sacrifice to You here on this mountain?* We aren't told

Abraham had those thoughts. We are told, instead, that he obeyed God without question. In fact, the New Testament gives us insight into what this father was thinking as he headed up the mountain with his young son to obey God's shocking request:

> It was *by faith* that Abraham offered Isaac as a sacrifice when God was testing him. Abraham, who had received God's promises, was ready to sacrifice his only son, Isaac, even though God had told him, "Isaac is the son through whom your descendants will be counted." Abraham *reasoned that if Isaac died, God was able to bring him back to life again.* And in a sense, Abraham did receive his son back from the dead (Hebrews 11:17-19 NLT).

It's important to realize that Abraham had probably never heard any accounts of people being resurrected from the dead. So for him to reason that *if Isaac died, God was able to bring him back to life again* indicates Abraham had pretty big faith and believed God was a pretty big God. Abraham knew that God had made a significant promise to him already—one that was foundational upon his son's birth and life and legacy. Abraham trusted that if God had given him Isaac to make him the father of nations and now God was asking for this son back, then obviously *God knew what He was doing.*

That kind of faith blows my mind. Again, Abraham didn't have the Scriptures to rely on or past stories to read of how God had come through for others in their lifetime. In fact, Abraham's test of faith ended up *becoming* part of the Scriptures, and his demonstration of faith in that test is one that we now learn from. Abraham, in his time of testing, had nothing else to go on but the personal promise God had made him. God gave Abraham His word. And that word was enough for this old man to conclude that *God knew what He was doing.*

With nothing else to go on but the character of God and belief in the integrity of His word, Abraham followed God's instructions. Upon reaching the top of the mountain, he bound his son's hands and feet and laid him on a stack of wood. He then raised a knife into the air and intending to bring it down into the warm flesh and beating heart of his long-awaited beloved son. Not until then did God quickly intervene, spare Isaac's life, and explain to Abraham that he had passed this heart-wrenching test:

> The angel of the LORD called to him from heaven and said, "Abraham, Abraham!" And he said, "Here I am." He said, "Do not stretch out your hand against the lad, and do nothing to him; for now I know that you fear God, since you have not withheld your son, your only son, from Me." Then Abraham raised his eyes and looked, and behold, behind him a ram caught in the thicket by his horns; and Abraham went and took the ram and offered him up for a burnt offering in the place of his son. Abraham called the name of that place The LORD Will Provide, as it is said to this day, "In the mount of the LORD it will be provided" (Genesis 22:11-14 NASB).

What Was God *Thinking*?

I remember my dad reading this story to me, from a children's Bible story book, when I was about seven years old. *How could God ask a father to do such a thing?* I remember thinking, and asking my dad. Even throughout my young adult years it was a difficult side of God for me to grasp. Only recently have I gained a more understanding glimpse into the heart and mind of God as I reflect on that incident, after which God reiterated His promise to Abraham to make him the father of nations and to bless all the nations of the world through him. I now realize that not only was God developing faith in a man upon whom He would build a nation, but He was fixing Abraham's heart on Him alone. God wanted Abraham to be willing to do whatever God asked of him. That's the kind of faith He looks for in us too.

And I can't help but think that God was looking for *one man* who would relate to His heart when His own Son would one day climb Mount Calvary and there be the sacrifice for the sins of all who would believe. Only Abraham would've known—at least momentarily—what it was like to offer up his beloved son as a sacrifice. Only Abraham would be able to relate to God's father heart in that unique way.

God asks us to partake of sacrifice—in small ways and sometimes in *huge* ways—because no other experience on earth will help us relate more to His heart. God knows what it is to have a broken heart after watching His righteous, innocent, beloved Son die to be the payment and propitiation for our sins. Don't ever think God doesn't understand any of the pain you have gone through. He made the ultimate sacrifice of what He loved the most, and He did it for you and me. We need to ask ourselves: Are *we* willing to give up what we love most…so that *God* can truly be first in our lives?

Hebrews 4:15 tells us that when Jesus lived and walked among us, He experienced the kind of pain we do. He was a man well acquainted with sorrows. He was tempted in the areas that we are, and yet He never sinned. Jesus demonstrated complete faith in His Father to get Him through all He experienced on this earth. And Jesus was obedient to His Father unto death. In fact, Jesus was familiar with more heartache and suffering than you and I will ever experience. So in that way, sacrifice helps us understand the heart of Jesus as well.

Hannah's Sacrifice

When Hannah made her vow to God, asking Him for a child that she would then give back to Him, she knew she had to deliver on that promise. When God faithfully "remembered her" and caused her to conceive, I'm sure she knew, from the moment she discovered a new life was growing within her womb, the seriousness of her vow and the importance of following through.

Look at how her story unfolds and feel her mother's heart as she rocks, feeds, and raises her only son those first few years, knowing the day will come all too soon when she will have to turn him over to the care of someone else. Her sacrifice—and ultimate test of faith—is yet to come:

> So in the course of time Hannah became pregnant and gave birth to a son. She named him Samuel, saying, "Because I asked the LORD for him."
>
> When her husband Elkanah went up with all his family to offer the annual sacrifice to the LORD and to fulfill his vow, Hannah did not go. She said to her husband, "After the boy is weaned, I will take him and present him before the LORD, and he will live there always."
>
> "Do what seems best to you," her husband Elkanah told her. "Stay here until you have weaned him; only may the LORD make good his word." So the woman stayed at home and nursed her son until she had weaned him.
>
> After he was weaned, she took the boy with her, young as he was, along with a three-year-old bull, an ephah of flour and a skin of wine, and brought him to the house of the LORD at Shiloh. When the bull had been sacrificed, they brought the boy to Eli, and she said to him, "Pardon me, my lord. As surely as you live, I am the woman who stood here beside you praying to the LORD. I prayed for this child, and the LORD has granted me what I asked of him. So now I give him to the LORD. For his whole life he will be given over to the LORD." And he worshiped the LORD there (1 Samuel 1:20-28).

Once Hannah received this son whom she had longed for and prayed for, she immediately remembered and proclaimed that her son belonged to the Lord. Hannah gave back to God what she wanted most, and she didn't see the rewards and blessings of that decision until years later.

If you're a mom reading this, I know that you are already wondering how Hannah could have possibly given up her son at such a young age. How could she bear bonding with her little guy knowing she would soon have to give him up? We can try to minimize Hannah's pain and position by thinking, *Well, she was giving him to the ministry, so that was better than just turning him over to anyone. She'd still see him yearly and check in on him and, besides, he'd have a safe, godly upbringing by being raised in the temple with the priests.* But keep in mind that Hannah was turning her child over to a *corrupt* priesthood. (Remember the reckless, immoral behavior of Eli's two sons, who were priests?) One Bible commentator said, "Into the defiled worship center she placed her very young, impressionable son. Although humanly it seemed to border on foolishness, this was an act of saintly sacrifice. Her commitment was to God; her gift was pre-arranged with Him. With prophetic insight she planted the next generation just as promised."[2]

Prior to giving up her son, Hannah had about three precious years with little Samuel, which was about the normal length of time Israelite mothers of that era spent weaning a child.[3] I imagine Hannah used that time wisely to instill in her little boy a spiritual foundation so he could stand strong while living in the corrupt house of Eli. Samuel was already walking and talking by the time Hannah brought him to his new home. He was at that age when children begin having "separation anxiety." While he was not old enough for kindergarten or preschool, little Samuel was old enough to have bonded with his mother. He was old enough to have been told of the significance of his life and of the God who would care for him.

It's very possible Hannah had the discernment to know that her son was going to the house of the priests at a crucial time in history...to make a crucial difference for the Lord and among His people. I imagine Hannah made every day with her young son count, knowing she would soon have to let go of his tiny hand, release him into God's care, and walk away to a childless home once again.

I imagine it was extremely difficult for Hannah to turn her son over to Eli and see him only once a year from then on, when she and Elkanah (and Peninnah, who now had nothing over Hannah) came to Shiloh to offer sacrifices to the Lord. They would've stayed in town only a few days at most, and that would have been the extent of Hannah's yearly involvement with her son as he was growing up. Scripture says she saw him each year and brought with her a little robe she had made for him (1 Samuel 2:19). During their short time together she could talk with him, remind him that he was her son, and affirm that God had a great plan for his life. And she could tell him that she prayed for him continually. Although her mothering took place from a distance, she could see him grow and continue to pray for his development. She could, year after year, see her dream of his life fulfilled.

Katherine, however, can no longer do *any* of those things.

The Sting of Sacrifice

Like Hannah, Katherine had to give up her son to God. But not in the way that any mother ever imagines she would have to.

Katherine's only child, Donald, was 22 years old and beginning his final semester at Auburn University in Alabama. He had a girlfriend, a job waiting for him upon graduation, and a promising future. So it shocked his mother, and everyone who knew him, when he was found dead on the floor of his apartment on August 18, 2012 from what police called "an apparent self-inflicted gunshot wound."

"We talked several times just a couple weeks before he died," Katherine said. "Each time we ended the conversation with 'I love you.' He seemed so happy and was telling me his plans for the weekend, and we agreed to speak later about how much his books would cost. I learned of his death through my brother-in-law, who saw it on Facebook! It took me hours to find out if he was dead and who to talk to as I waited for deputies to come see me. To this day, no one can understand why he would take his life."

Not only did Katherine lose her beloved son, she is left without answers—with a situation that makes no sense to her at all. As the police investigated Donald's death, no problems surfaced, and they found no evidence of anything that would be a reason for him to take his life. Donald had no history of drug use, depression, or even mood changes. He had many friends and future plans. The detective investigating the matter was perplexed, but had no explanation. Katherine was never able to see a toxicology report or autopsy report. She was left with so many questions, including why Donald's back door was unlocked, why his wallet was missing and then turned in anonymously later, and why his cell phone was never found. And if he really wanted to take his life, it didn't make sense to her that he would've left without saying good-bye.

"My son and I were very close," Katherine said. "If he had planned to do this, he would've told me why. He would've at least left a note. Whichever way he went, he's now gone from this earth. I have to learn to live with that more than try to figure out why this happened. My son, my only son, whom I struggled to keep from being born prematurely and raised mainly by myself, is dead. He was the light of my life. We were so close and he was on the verge of an exciting part of his life. That now is lost to both of us."

Katherine, who has lost her father, her grandparents, and close friends, said, "Nothing hurts as much as the loss of a child.

"It feels as if whole parts of my body and soul have been ripped from me. At times I feel like I can't breathe, and the tears come fast and furious at unexpected moments. I have been told by other mothers who have gone through this that it is not going to get better for a long time, and that there is no such thing as normal again.

It will be a new normal and I will be a new 'Katherine.' What was, is no more. It really seems as if the pain increases as time goes by. At times I feel paralyzed with grief."

And yet she trusts that *God knows what He is doing.*

Katherine has known and heard of women who have lost children and become so devastated and so angry with God that they've questioned their faith—and even walked away from it.

"I don't understand how anyone can continue onward if they don't have the hope they'll see their loved ones in heaven," she said. "What I've gone through is horrible. It's the worst thing a parent can experience. But to turn one's back on God and go through it alone would be far worse. I haven't lost my faith through this. It has only made me stronger.

"Although this is the worst thing I've ever experienced, I have a living hope and One to help me get *through* it. I will never get *over* this, but I can get *through* it."

As a mother, I can't imagine the tears Katherine has cried. I can't imagine the ache of wanting to see and hug and hold and laugh with my child again, knowing that will not happen again this side of heaven. I've been told one can never understand the depth of pain involved in losing a child until they do. And I *pray* I never will. But as I think of that horrible possibility it takes me to the cross, where my heavenly Father willingly—for my sake and yours—gave up His Son so He would not be eternally separated from you and me. Perhaps the only comfort to the mom who has had to bury her child is the comfort that there is One who completely understands her pain because He has gone into that same situation before her and *because of* her.

Giving It Back to God

God will sometimes ask us to give something to Him that we are reluctant to give up—to grow our dependence on Him, and to shape us for His eternal purposes.

"Faith by its very nature must be tested and tried," says Oswald Chambers. "And the real trial of faith is not that we find it difficult to trust God, but that God's character must be proven as trustworthy in our own minds."[4]

Our faith is tried when we are asked to give something back to God that was never ours in the first place. Our faith is tried when we are called upon to trust in the character of God even though what He is asking seems impossible, hurtful, or unfair.

Alena, from chapter 2, remembers the point at which God asked for her sacrifice—the surrender of her husband, Rick, who was dying of lymphoma.

"There were a lot of conversations I had with God while driving to the hospital every day to be with Rick," Alena said. "Everyone was praying. They were all praying for his healing. Everyone told me he was going to be healed. But something inside of me said he wouldn't be healed. I finally told the Lord, 'You can have him.' After seeing Rick decline I came to terms with reality and said, 'Lord, he's Yours. You gave him to me for a short time. I was blessed—beyond blessed—to be his wife. But he's Yours, and if this is what You choose, so be it.'

"I had to then comfort everyone else," Alena said. "People were angry with God. They were devastated." But Alena was able to maintain her strength because she realized to whom her husband belonged. He was God's, and now, God was taking him back.

"I remember the doctor telling me the story of a little boy sitting at his mother's feet and looking up at her as she worked on a needlepoint project. He asked her what she was doing because it didn't look good from his viewpoint. His mother told him, 'When I'm finished, you're going to see how beautiful this is.'

"That's how it is with God," Alena said. "We only see the ugliness of our present situation when we're being called to surrender. We don't see the beauty of the end result He is working toward."

Laying It on the Altar

Perhaps as you're reading this, God is asking you to release something to Him. A fear? A reservation? Something you're holding onto with clenched fists because You are afraid He may take it from you? Dear friend, God is not the one who gives us a spirit of fear (2 Timothy 1:7). He does not look for areas in which He can hurt you so that you will be a stronger follower of His. I would venture to say that He has eternal purposes that are beyond our understanding and He knows who can handle those losses and grow stronger through them and who cannot. Be one whom God knows will love Him and trust Him regardless of the cost.

Here are some ways you can lay on the altar all that you have as a way of saying, "Because You gave it all for me, I want to respond, in faith, by giving it all for You." It doesn't mean God will take from you what you love the most. Rather, it means He will give you His peace so that no matter what happens in this life, you will not be shaken.

1. Realize God knows what He's doing. Herein lies absolute trust. And comfort. To not understand why, but to fully trust His decision is how we show God—and others— that we realize He knows what He is doing. Like Alena and Amanda and Dawn—who all saw their husbands slip into eternity—the key was knowing, without a doubt, that God knew what He was doing. As happened with Katherine, who can cling to God in spite of the pain from losing her son, the key is trusting God even when you don't have all the answers. When you can say, "God, Your will not mine," you have passed through the first step of surrender.

> When you can say, "God, Your will not mine," you have passed through the first step of surrender.

2. Remember He wants what's best for you. You may have to keep reminding yourself of three things: (1) God is good; (2) God cannot do anything that is not in accordance with His loving kindness; (3) God knows better than you what is not just good, but the very best for your life. If you can trust Him with that, you are trusting Him in the dark. And that is true faith.

3. *Release to Him your fears, expectations, and desires.* You and I don't need to stress out or lose sleep over the situations we can't work out. When we turn our fears, concerns, expectations, and plans of how we would've worked things out over to God, we are saying, "God, You can manage my life far better than I can, and I trust You with all that I am and all that I have." If God can hold the entire universe together, He can keep and preserve you even when it seems your world is falling apart.

Whatever the Cost

In the devotional *My Utmost for His Highest*, Oswald Chambers posed this question that continues to convict my heart:

> Am I fully prepared to allow God to grip me by His power and do a work in me that is truly worthy of Himself? Sanctification is not my idea of what I want God to do for me—sanctification is God's idea of what He wants to do for me. But He has to get me into the state of mind and spirit where I will allow Him to sanctify me completely, whatever the cost (1 Thess. 5:23-24).[5]

That phrase "whatever the cost" can be scary at times. But you and I don't need to fear a God who loves us unconditionally and sent His Son to die for us. We need to, instead, trust Him—as Hannah did—with all that He has given us. What we place into His hands is safer there than if we put it anywhere else on this earth.

Chambers, who challenged me with his question above, also comforted me with these words about our God who showed such enormous sacrificial love for us:

At times God will appear like an unkind friend, but He is not; He will appear like an unnatural father, but He is not; He will appear like an unjust judge, but He is not. Keep the thought that the mind of God is behind all things strong and growing. Not even the smallest detail of life happens unless God's will is behind it. Therefore you can rest in perfect confidence in Him.[6]

Faith, as the Bible teaches it, is faith in God coming against everything that contradicts Him—a faith that says, "I will remain true to God's character whatever He may do." The highest and the greatest expression of faith in the Bible is—(Job's statement after he lost everything most dear to him) "Though He slay me, yet will I trust Him" (Job 13:15).[7]

Go ahead, my friend. You can do it. Loosen your grip on what you have held onto so tightly. Offer it back to your loving Savior with an open hand. And sense His pleasure in the peace that sweeps over your soul when you have finally come to that place He has been waiting for *all* of your life.

Giving It Up for His Glory

Apply the three Rs—realize, remember, release—to your situation by writing a prayerful response to God in the spaces below:

Step One: God, I *realize* You know what You are doing when it comes to _____

_____ .

Step Two: God, help me *remember* that You know what is best for me and therefore _____

_____ .

Step Three: God, I *release* to You _____

_____

and I trust that You _____

_____ .

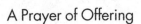

A Prayer of Offering

Now take those sentences above and make them your prayer to God, offering back to Him what you long for most.

Continuing On

When You Remain Faithful

Each year his mother made him a little robe and took it to him
when she went up with her husband to offer the annual sacrifice.

1 Samuel 2:19

It's been said that a true test of our character is who we are when we're alone.

I would add that our character is truly tested when the road ahead is uncertain, when the path we walk is painful, when our diagnosis is terminal.

I met Ellen while speaking at a weekend women's conference in New York. Her warm smile was inviting, so I sat down next to her at the lunch table. I introduced myself to her, a soft-spoken woman whose eyes shone and said, "God is *so* good."

I had just heard that same phrase from Alena (whose two-time cancer story is told in chapter 2), so I asked Ellen to tell me her story.

"I've been surgically glued, screwed, stapled, and sewn back together," she said with a smile.

A smile?

Curious, I leaned in closer, and she told me the rest of her story.

"I have terminal blood cancer," Ellen continued. "*Terminal*...what a funny word. A terminal is where trains meet, so I'm just passing through, I guess."

I wasn't fully prepared for what Ellen went on to tell me. You don't often meet a woman who will talk so freely—and peacefully—about her impending death. But I was so glad that I asked. If I hadn't, I would've missed my opportunity to meet a legacy in the making.

Ellen has been diagnosed with multiple myeloma, a blood cancer for which there is no cure. "For others with cancer a tumor grows," Ellen said. "For me, my blood is eating my bones...it creates holes, fractures, and lesions. To a bone specialist, it's sort of like advanced osteoporosis."

Doctors gave Ellen up to ten years left to live. She spent the first year trying to survive the cancer treatments—two major surgeries, six months of chemotherapy, and a stem cell transplant.

Ellen has two daughters—a developmentally delayed 28-year-old and an 18-year-old (who was 15 when Ellen was diagnosed).

"My older daughter is settled into a wonderful Christian group home. I'm at peace with her care. But it's leaving my teenager, Mary, that breaks my heart," she said. "My oncologist told me that I needed to write three letters for Mary—one for her to read at her high school graduation, one for her to read at her college graduation, and the third for her to read on her wedding day in case I didn't make it the ten years."

Just as Hannah must have wrestled with eventually leaving her son in the care of Eli, Ellen wrestles with leaving her youngest daughter, Mary, when God takes her from this earth.

"She and I have always been close. I wonder if I'll see her walk across the stage to get her diploma. I wonder who she will become. I wonder if I've met her husband or if the Lord will bring someone else into her life. I wonder what mistakes she'll make where she'll need a mother to help her through. Will I still be here for her?"

A Certain Peace

Although Ellen is uncertain how much longer she has to live, she, like Dawn and Katherine from the last chapter, is certain that *God knows what He is doing.*

"I had a choice," Ellen said. "I could be angry with God and go through this miserably. Or I could companion with God and go through it His way. I was going to go through it anyway, regardless of how I chose to. I wanted a closer walk with Him because I couldn't do it alone."

Like Hannah of the Bible, Ellen has poured her heart out to God. Her request was originally for healing and for length of days so she can be involved in more of her daughter's life. But so far, rather than a yes, God has given her the answer of Himself.

"God doesn't owe me a yes answer to my prayers," Ellen said, "but His promise is that He will never leave me nor forsake me [Hebrews 13:5]. He will walk with me through this. Being in God's perfect will, even if it's not where we want to be, is the best place for us.

"In the beginning, I would wake up with the fear of *I am going to die,*" she said. "One morning I woke up and cried out, 'God, give me back my joy.' The morning when God helped me realize that I had never *lost* my joy was a turning point in accepting my diagnosis.

"It so happened that after I asked God to give me back my joy, in my devotional that morning I read, 'The joy of the Lord is my strength.' I realized then that I was looking at things all wrong. I then asked God to change my thoughts. What came into my mind at that point was the realization that *I am greatly loved*—by God. Yes, others expressed their love for me and later I would be overwhelmed by their love, but this particular day (and every day since) I was given a glimpse of *God's* heart toward me. So my prayer was that my thought each day would be that *I am greatly loved.* And sure enough, the next morning, my first thought when I woke up was *I am greatly loved.*

"The knowledge that God greatly loves me…delights my soul beyond expression."

"For the first time in my life I realized that God *delighted* in me, and it's not because of anything I've done. He delights in each one of us. He never wants us to feel alone, forsaken, or hopeless. He wants us to know that deep love that delights in us and cares for each concern in our lives.

"The knowledge that God delights in His relationship with me has made me enjoy my relationship with Him more than I had previously thought possible. Prior to my diagnosis I hadn't a clue as to how to enjoy God. But the knowledge that God greatly loves me, and that I bring Him pleasure and joy simply by being His, delights my soul beyond expression. It has given me a heavenly perspective and a healthy anticipation for heaven. Imagine what would happen if all of us had that thought as we faced each day."

Ellen continues to be faithful to God by teaching Bible classes, speaking to women's groups and sharing her story, and considering each day a precious one in which she can live for Him.

"I used to think that the time I had left in my life was short. My friend comforted me recently by telling me, 'No, Ellen, your life is exactly the amount of time it was appointed to be.' I found comfort in that."

What She Has Gained

"Perhaps the missing piece for me was thinking that life here on earth could be the prize instead of fully understanding that the prize is Jesus Christ Himself—the King of kings and Lord of lords. He is the hope of glory. He has taken the sting out of death and even given that a purpose. As Paul said, 'To me, to live is Christ and to die is gain' [Philippians 1:21].

"Another missing piece in my life was a full understanding of the importance of a growing faith and trust in the Lord. I've come to believe that the Lord longs for us to trust Him and will use anything to get us to a point where we will say, 'Above all things I love You. You are a good God.' He grows our trust by using what we consider to be tragedies. I believe, to Him, they are opportunities for us to get to know Him better. For when we trust God with all of our 'stuff' (including our hopes, dreams, and fears), we then can see how

He opens the floodgates of heaven and meets our every need with blessings upon blessings."

Unlike Ellen, I've never been diagnosed with cancer. Unlike Katherine in the last chapter, I've never suffered the loss of a child. Unlike Alena and Amanda and Dawn, whose stories you've read in previous chapters, I've never experienced the pain of losing a husband. At the time of this writing, I haven't yet lost my parents or any siblings, or my home due to financial hardship or natural disaster. And yet in the day that one or more of those things do happen, I can only pray that my response will be like Ellen's—and that of God's servant Job: "The LORD gave and the LORD has taken away; may the name of the LORD be praised" (Job 1:21).

Hannah's Song of Celebration

Hannah saw the Lord give and take away in her life. She prayed for a child, received him from the Lord, and when he was weaned, she gave him back to the Lord. Scripture tells us that after she brought little Samuel to Eli she did something that I find to be so amazing—she sang a song of *praise* to God! Her song of thanksgiving focused on the Lord's sovereignty and His grace to the humble, as well as His deliverance and the way He reverses the fortunes of those who are boastful and those who wait on Him. (Could she be referring to that pest, Peninnah, when she says, "She who has had many sons pines away"? Just a thought.) Listen to the words of this woman who is thanking God for giving her a long-awaited son *even as* she is giving him back to the Lord for the rest of his life.

Then Hannah prayed and said:

> My heart rejoices in the LORD;
> in the LORD my horn is lifted high.
> My mouth boasts over my enemies,
> for I delight in your deliverance.

There is no one holy like the LORD;
    there is no one besides you;
    there is no Rock like our God.

Do not keep talking so proudly
    or let your mouth speak such arrogance,
for the LORD is a God who knows,
    and by him deeds are weighed.

The bows of the warriors are broken,
    but those who stumbled are armed with strength.
Those who were full hire themselves out for food,
    but those who were hungry are hungry no more.
She who was barren has borne seven children,
    but she who has had many sons pines away.

The LORD brings death and makes alive;
    he brings down to the grave and raises up.
The LORD sends poverty and wealth;
    he humbles and he exalts.
He raises the poor from the dust
    and lifts the needy from the ash heap;
he seats them with princes
    and has them inherit a throne of honor.

For the foundations of the earth are the LORD's;
    on them he has set the world.
He will guard the feet of his faithful servants,
    but the wicked will be silenced in the place of
        darkness.

It is not by strength that one prevails;
    those who oppose the LORD will be broken.
The Most High will thunder from heaven;
    the LORD will judge the ends of the earth.

He will give strength to his king
and exalt the horn of his anointed
(1 Samuel 2:1-10).

The words and songs of the people back in the Bible days can sound very different from how we talk today. So I looked up Hannah's song of celebration in a modern translation that still takes into account the meaning of the original Hebrew words Hannah used in her song, but adds in the emotion of the Hebrew language and expresses it in the way we would say it today. I was so moved by it when I read through it that I wanted you to have that experience too. Read it now, again, and feel the jubilation in this woman's heart— not at what she had to give up, but at what God was doing in her through her surrender. See if this doesn't sound like something *you* can sing as you see Him come through for you:

I'm bursting with God-news!
     I'm walking on air.
I'm laughing at my rivals.
     I'm dancing my salvation.
Nothing and no one is holy like God,
     no rock mountain like our God.
Don't dare talk pretentiously—
     not a word of boasting, ever!
For God knows what's going on.
     He takes the measure of everything that happens.
The weapons of the strong are smashed to pieces,
     while the weak are infused with fresh strength.
The well-fed are out begging in the streets for crusts,
     while the hungry are getting second helpings.
The barren woman has a houseful of children,
     while the mother of many is bereft.
God brings death and God brings life,
     brings down to the grave and raises up.

> GOD brings poverty and GOD brings wealth;
>   he lowers, he also lifts up.
> He puts poor people on their feet again;
>   he rekindles burned-out lives with fresh hope,
> Restoring dignity and respect to their lives—
>   a place in the sun!
> For the very structures of earth are GOD's;
>   he has laid out his operations on a firm foundation.
> He protectively cares for his faithful friends, step by
>   step,
>   but leaves the wicked to stumble in the dark.
>   No one makes it in this life by sheer muscle!
> GOD's enemies will be blasted out of the sky,
>   crashed in a heap and burned.
> GOD will set things right all over the earth,
>   he'll give strength to his king,
>   he'll set his anointed on top of the world! (MSG).

Oh, to have a heart of praise like that on the heels of sacrifice. It is then that we are living out God's will for us as stated in 1 Thessalonians 5:18: "In *everything* give thanks; for this is God's will for you in Christ Jesus" (NASB). What I love the most about Hannah's song is that it isn't a sad song recounting all she was giving up. It is a song of anticipation and celebration of all that God will do with what she's just given Him. Oh, that you and I can have that kind of expectation—rather than regret—when we surrender to God what we love the most.

Hannah's Continued Faithfulness

After Hannah sang her song of praise and went home, she didn't just move on with her life. She continued to hold her son in her heart as any mother would. Year after year she returned with her husband to Shiloh to offer sacrifices to the Lord. And each time, Hannah brought to her son a robe she had made for him to wear during the next year that they would be apart. I imagine that as she sewed together each robe, she sowed prayers for his heart and his growing character and integrity too.

Scripture tells us how God honored Hannah for her continual faithfulness to her son and to the Lord:

> Samuel was ministering before the LORD—a boy wearing a linen ephod. Each year his mother made him a little robe and took it to him when she went up with her husband to offer the annual sacrifice. Eli would bless Elkanah and his wife, saying, "May the LORD give you children by this woman to take the place of the one she prayed for and gave to the LORD." Then they would go home. And the LORD was gracious to Hannah; she gave birth to three sons and two daughters. Meanwhile, the boy Samuel grew up in the presence of the LORD (1 Samuel 2:18-21).

God rewarded Hannah's faithfulness to Him by giving her *five* more children! But He also blessed Samuel's life. Later in the story we are told something very significant about Hannah's firstborn son: "The child Samuel grew in stature, and in favor both with the LORD and men" (verse 26 NKJV).

That same description, almost word for word, is given to only one other person in the Bible. In Luke 2:52 we see those basic words applied to Jesus' childhood: "Jesus grew in wisdom and stature, and in favor with God and man."

Samuel had the anointing of God and grew up with the same kind of favor that God bestowed on His own Son. This description of Samuel is another indication that Hannah was faithful in her continued prayers for him and the contact she had with him every year. We will see more of this in the final chapter when we talk about Hannah's—and Samuel's—legacy.

Anyone can be faithful for a moment, or when times are good.

But to be faithful to God for a lifetime no matter what storms blow in and out of our lives? That is what God smiles on. That is what builds our legacy.

Pam's Ongoing Struggle

During her 40-year walk with God, Pam has faced one incident after another that could have rocked her faith. One storm after another has beat upon her door. Yet she has remained faithful, even during times of the utmost uncertainty.

When Pam was 35 years old (and the mother of eight children by then!) she had a routine mammogram and a doctor visit because of an unusual menstrual period. When she got the call about the tests, the news was exciting and terrifying, all at the same time. She was pregnant with her ninth child! That was the exciting part, she said. But her mammogram showed breast cancer! Her first reaction was panic. She couldn't take treatment for cancer while carrying a child. But if she refused treatment she could die. Her mind swirled with all the terrifying "what ifs" that every mother with a diagnosis asks. For her, the nagging question was this: What about my eight— maybe nine children—if I die?

Even though Pam has a husband whom she knows would take good care of her children if she were to die, she still worried about missing their lives and not being there for them.

"I spent the next few days running everything through my mind, fearing death while being conscious of the new life within me," she said. "Through reading my Bible, crying, and seeking the Lord for an answer, He brought peace to my heart."

Pam believed God's answer to her was to do nothing—just trust Him and rest in Him for His perfect will. "I was convinced that no matter what happened, all would be okay."

Pam drew strength from many of the songs in Scripture, including Psalm 37:3-5:

Trust in the LORD and do good;
> dwell in the land and enjoy safe pasture.
Take delight in the LORD,
> and he will give you the desires of your heart.
Commit your way to the LORD;
> trust in him and he will do this.

"The promises in God's Word are true and will never fail," Pam said. "I held onto this scripture, and several others, as I waited for the results of the biopsy." The day the results returned, Pam was told that the radiologist just shook her head and said, "I don't understand; I was certain this was cancer, but it isn't." Pam says, "My friend from church, who worked with the radiologist, said 'I know what happened. We prayed for her at church and God answered our prayers for her healing. It's a miracle.'"

Then, when Pam was in her mid-forties, she became ill with multiple symptoms lasting six to eight weeks at a time. This happened twice, each time a year-and-a-half apart (the second time being much worse than the first). Her arms and legs felt extremely weak, her fingers tingled and were numb. She had difficulty holding things without dropping them. Her speech was slurred and her thought process was hindered. She had no energy and during the second episode, her legs dragged behind her when she walked. After an MRI, she was diagnosed with multiple sclerosis.

"I had ten children, with eight still at home, and lived in a three-story house. At that time, I had a friend at church with MS. Her MS progressed rapidly until she was in a wheelchair; but then she took some new medications that stopped that progression for a time. I wanted to get started on the medication immediately so I could avoid becoming crippled, but I could not get a neurologist to

"I told Him that if He could use me better in a wheelchair than standing, then so be it."

confirm the diagnosis. I was so discouraged and spent my days crying and in turmoil. One day, about five weeks into the second episode, the Lord showed me that my battle was not with the doctors, but with Him.

"He wanted me to surrender to His perfect will, even if that meant being crippled the rest of my life. I really wanted the Lord to use me and I longed for His peace and joy once again. After a time of crying out and struggling, I surrendered my will to whatever God had for my future. I told Him that if He could use me better in a wheelchair than standing, then so be it. I was immediately filled with His peace and joy."

Shortly after her surrender, Pam found a doctor whom she said began to *really* listen. God then raised Pam up from that illness within a few weeks. Her symptoms never returned.

"God used this severe situation in my life to teach me that I can trust Him no matter what I face. His will is perfect no matter what the outcome. My longing is to be used of the Lord in some way, but it is up to the Lord how He wants to do that. The faith of so many people in our church, who prayed for me during these times, was strengthened throughout this whole trial.

"Looking back now, I was trying to protect myself from being crippled instead of resting in God's perfect will for how *He* wanted to use my life."

Her Greatest Trial Yet

Five years ago, when Pam was 55 years old, she experienced the most difficult struggle of her life. Her 17-year-old daughter, Naomi (the youngest of her ten children), drove through a flashing red light and was t-boned on the driver's side of her small truck by another driver going 55 miles per hour. Naomi was flown to the hospital by helicopter with broken ribs, a torn diaphragm, a collapsed lung, a broken pelvis, and severe brain injury.

Pam said that as Naomi lay unconscious in the intensive care unit, the family didn't know from day to day whether she would live or die.

"I was haunted every night by some words I had spoken a number of times in the recent past. I had raised children for thirty-four years now and was ready to be done. I longed for the day when I would be free to do what I wanted, and I would say to my friends, 'When Naomi gets married and I finally have an empty nest, I am going to throw a party and invite everyone.' But with Naomi in the hospital, I suddenly realized my parenting might be over sooner than I had expected. I cried out to the Lord for forgiveness and asked Him to raise Naomi up.

"God did forgive me, of course. I praised Him that He doesn't hold our sins against us, but that as we confess our sins to Him, He is merciful and forgiving (Psalm 130:1-4). He reminded me that He gives us our precious children for such a short time to love, train in His Word, teach to love Him, and prepare for future independence. He reminded me how much my children are a treasure to me. His answer to raising her up was 'Wait—it is going to be a long road.'

"Knowing that I had forgiveness and peace with the Lord, I was able to wait on Him and trust Him for whatever His perfect will was for Naomi. Throughout the entire trial, God was faithful to me, providing for every need along the way and filling me with strength and peace.

"So many times over the last five years I have cried out to the Lord with Naomi. Most of the time, it was because I had taken my eyes off of Him and allowed myself to dwell on my circumstances. But today, when I look back at what has happened, I can see how the Lord has grown my faith over the years and prepared me for this present trial."

How did Pam stay strong in her faith in spite of all that has occurred to her over the past two decades? She continued to cling to God's promises and constantly draws strength from Scripture.

Staying Faithful During the Journey

Hannah remained faithful to God year in and year out and honored her commitment to Him. Similarly, Ellen and Pam have stayed faithful to God as well. With their examples in mind, I want to leave you with some thoughts about how *you* can stay strong and faithful through the struggles in your life.

Surround Yourself with Scripture

Ellen has found guidance for her situation, day by day, in Scripture: "God doesn't tell us to be thankful *for* our circumstances, but to be thankful *in* them" (see 1 Thessalonians 5:18). As she practiced gratefulness in all things, she eventually was able to truly thank the Lord for the "gifts" that at one time were difficult to accept. "Now I can thank Him for the cancer, but initially that wasn't the case," she said.

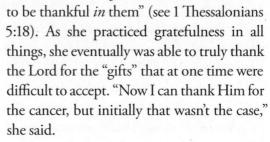

> The more you read and hear and study *His* words...the more you will be encouraged and enabled to remain faithful.

Scripture has been a huge comfort to Pam as well—particularly during the time she carried a baby and believed she had cancer, and in these uncertain days as she cares for her youngest child. Do you have certain verses hidden in your heart (that is, memorized), posted in front of you on paper, worn around your wrist on a bracelet? The more you read and hear and study *His* words—rather than the words of others—the more you will be encouraged and enabled to remain faithful.

Soak in His presence

Ellen found that focusing on God's presence (and Scripture that reminds her of His presence) has comforted her during uncertain days.

"The blessings in my life have to do with God's presence. The awareness of His continual presence and great love for me sustain me. It's not a love I deserve, but a love He freely lavishes on me. It's a love that keeps my perspective toward heaven. He has lifted me above my circumstances. Along the way, verses from His Word have come alive. His promise to never leave me nor forsake me has been a balm [Hebrews 13:5 and Isaiah 43:2-3]. Psalm 145:18-19 says that He is near to all who call upon Him, and He will fulfill my desire and hear my cry. I know I can trust His promises because He says in Psalm 145:13 that He is trustworthy in all His promises and faithful in all He does. In Isaiah 41:10 and 13, He has assured me that He will strengthen me and help me and uphold me with His righteous right hand. I don't even have to extend that hand. He takes hold of my hand for me and tells me not to fear. I have known all these verses for years, but now they are more personal to me because the Lord speaks them to me to encourage me. He speaks them to me because He loves me and wants to help me to finish well."

See Jesus as the Prize

Ellen says, "God's answer to me is that He is enough for both me and my loved ones. Psalm 16:11 says, 'You will show me the path of life. In Your presence is fullness of joy; at Your right hand are pleasures forever more.'[1] Life on this side of eternity is not the prize. *Jesus* is the prize! Jesus is showing me how to walk through the valley of the shadow of death by the light of His presence. And I've learned that where there is a shadow, there is a light."

When our life's goal is success, or to achieve a dream, or to have something we so desire, our happiness may be contingent on whether or not we receive what we prize. But when *Jesus* is our prize, God assures us in His Word that we will receive that prize we are longing for: "You will seek Me and find Me when you search for Me with all your heart" (Jeremiah 29:13 NASB).

It's Your Turn

Now it's your turn. You've read of how Ellen has praised God in spite of a disease that is ravaging her body. You've read about how Pam continues to look to God as the giver of blessings in spite of what could be seen as bitter in her life. What about you? How will you continue on so that God can do what He desires in your life—build in you a legacy?

Staying Faithful in the Struggle

Read through the following passages of Scripture that spoke encouragement to Pam during her struggles and highlight the ones that speak personally to you about remaining faithful when you otherwise feel like giving up.

Psalm 62:5-8

> My soul, wait silently for God alone,
> For my expectation is from Him.
> He only is my rock and my salvation;
> He is my defense;
> I shall not be moved.
> In God is my salvation and my glory;
> The rock of my strength,
> And my refuge, is in God.
>
> Trust in Him at all times, you people;
> Pour out your heart before Him;
> God is a refuge for us (NKJV).

Psalm 118:8

> It is better to take refuge in the LORD
> Than to trust in man (NASB).

Proverbs 3:5-6

> Trust in the LORD with all your heart
> And do not lean on your own understanding.
> In all your ways acknowledge Him,
> And He will make your paths straight (NASB).

Psalm 130:1-4

> Out of the depths I cry to you, LORD;
>> Lord, hear my voice.
> Let your ears be attentive
>> to my cry for mercy.
>
> If you, LORD, kept a record of sins,
>> Lord, who could stand?
> But with you there is forgiveness,
>> so that we can, with reverence, serve you (NIV).

A Prayer for Pressing On

Lord God,

I want to be a woman who clings to You at all times, not just when I need something from You. May I never grow complacent because life is going well. And may I never turn my back on You because of pain I don't understand. I want to be one who pleases Your heart by remaining faithful to You through thick and thin.

I have not arrived at the place where I truly want to be spiritually, "but one thing I do: forgetting what lies behind and reaching forward to what lies ahead, I press on toward the goal for the prize of the upward call of God in Christ Jesus" (Philippians 3:13-14 NASB).

Lord, give me the strength to continue on in my faith and trust in You.

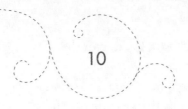

10

Looking Ahead

When Your Longing—or Loss—
Becomes a Legacy

The LORD was gracious to Hannah; she gave birth
to three sons and two daughters. Meanwhile, the
boy Samuel grew up in the presence of the LORD.

1 SAMUEL 2:21

Alejandra was thrilled when she and her husband discovered—on the day of their fifth wedding anniversary—that she was pregnant with their second child.

With excitement, she shared the news with her parents and siblings during a family get-together. Amidst the congratulations and celebration, she remembers sensing some hesitancy on the part of her younger sister.

"I would later learn that she was also pregnant but she had been experiencing complications and the doctors weren't sure if it was going to be a viable pregnancy," Alejandra explained. "I provided her with support and told her I would be praying for her. Thankfully, the tests came back with good news and for a few weeks we were both pregnant at the same time with due dates that were only days apart. It was an exciting time!"

And then, it was as if the roles reversed. Alejandra began experiencing complications with her pregnancy, culminating with the dreaded phone call from her doctor that confirmed she was having a miscarriage.

"I remember thinking, *How could this be happening to me?* Even though I had the miscarriage early on, that did not mean I had not grown attached to the baby, that I hadn't already started to dream about what this baby would be like," Alejandra said. "It felt unreal when it happened. You never think it will happen to you."

At that point, Alejandra entered a deep, dark tunnel of pain that many women experience after losing an unborn or newborn child. "I prayed to God to take the pain away. I would cry in my car and when I was alone. I would cry during worship time at church. I asked people to pray for me. It took some time, but little by little, I started to heal.

"God's *no* might simply be a *wait*."

"On one particular Sunday, during a baby dedication service, God used my pastor to speak healing words to me. A couple who was dedicating their baby boy shared that she'd had four miscarriages before finally giving birth to a son. And through all of that, she never lost faith that God would one day give her a baby. From the pulpit, she shared that she had found comfort in 1 Samuel 1:20:

> In the course of time Hannah became pregnant and gave birth to a son. She named him Samuel, saying, 'Because I asked the LORD for him.'

"That verse gave me a lot of strength too," Alejandra said. "The pastor went on to say, 'I know some of you are still going through this. And I want you to know that you may think that God is telling you *no*. But God's *no* might simply be a *wait*.'

"This brought me a lot of comfort," Alejandra continued. "Our pastor also mentioned that even though we might know we have to wait, it won't necessarily make life any easier, and we are still going to hurt, *but that is why our God is the God of all comfort* [see 2 Corinthians 1:3].

"That is when I found the Bible verse that comforted me the most during that time."

The Day It Started to Make Sense

Because Alejandra's sister had a due date just days away from when Alejandra's baby would have been born, Alejandra was concerned about any mixed emotions she might feel upon meeting her sister's new baby. "I had hoped that I would at least be pregnant again by the time my little niece arrived. But God had said, 'No, you must wait.'"

When Alejandra received the call from her sister that the baby had arrived, she and her husband made the two-hour drive to meet the newest addition to the family.

"My husband held my hand during the drive and asked me if I was okay. I told him yes, and I truly was. It was incredibly special and joyous to meet little Catalina, my sister's first baby. When I left the hospital that day I felt good and I was hopeful that one day God would finally say yes to my heart's desire to have another baby."

After Alejandra arrived home that night, she received an email from her best friend, Kelly. Kelly had told her that she had a good friend named Stephanie who lived out of state and had just experienced a miscarriage. Kelly had asked Alejandra to reach out to Stephanie with words of encouragement.

"I thought it was pretty amazing that I would receive this request on *this* day, the same day I met my sister's new baby. I was unsure of how I might handle it because of the loss I had been through. And it was the same day that God had confirmed to me that He had healed my heart of the loss by the way I reacted to my sister's new baby."

Alejandra stayed up into the early hours of the morning to compose an email for Stephanie, whom she did not know. In the subject line, she wrote, "You are in my prayers":

…So now 8 months later, I feel in my heart that one day the Lord will give me a second child. I will continue to wait patiently for Him to fulfill this desire in my heart, as He did with our first child. I trust that it will happen when it is God's will. I feel as if He is "working out" a testimony in me, but I still don't know how it will end yet. Also, I don't think it's any minor coincidence that I'm receiving this email today. I like to think of coincidences as God-engineered moments. Today, I became an aunt for the first time and I met my niece at the hospital. After my miscarriage, I was unsure of the mixed emotions I might feel upon meeting my niece because my sister's baby arrived around the same time that my child would have been born. But today was incredibly special. Over the past few months, I had been hoping that I would be pregnant again by the time my niece arrived because I didn't know if I would be fully healed from the experience I had gone through.

We're still not pregnant…but the very happy and joyful visit at the hospital today showed me just how much God has healed me and how much strength He has given me. And I know, Stephanie, that *He will do the same for you* because He is "the Father of compassion and the God of all comfort" (2 Corinthians 1:3).

"And that is when it hit me," Alejandra said. "I had pulled out my Bible to make sure I was precise in quoting 2 Corinthians 1:3, and that is when the next verse caught my attention. I hadn't noticed it before, but now it stood out to me as if it were in big, bold letters written especially for me that night. Through tears, I read the last part of 2 Corinthians 1:3 and the next verse over and over again: '…the God of all comfort, *who comforts us in all our troubles, so that we can comfort those in any trouble with the comfort we ourselves receive from God.*'

"I could not contain my tears of joy and laughter," Alejandra exclaimed. "I had one of those awesome, personal God moments that can only come from experiencing pain and then His amazing healing touch. I then realized perhaps it was in God's infinite wisdom that He had decided that I wouldn't be pregnant just yet so that I could see that I had been healed from the pain of my loss."

Five months after Alejandra sent that email to Stephanie, she learned that she was pregnant again. Nine months later she gave birth to Esteban, a healthy baby boy.

"My best friend Kelly gave birth to her second baby boy eleven days after me, which had also been a request of mine to God ('If I can't be pregnant with my sister, can I be pregnant at the same time as my best friend, Kelly?'); and Stephanie gave birth to her fourth child two weeks after Kelly. God is so good!"

God saw Alejandra's tears back when He had said, "Wait" and she heard it as "No." And He saw her faithfulness in trusting Him even though she didn't receive what she had asked. Today, He sees her joy—and hears her praise—as she comforts and encourages others because of the pain He has brought her through. And throughout eternity, perhaps you and I will see glimpses of how God has turned our losses into a legacy.

Fixing Our Eyes Forward

What if—at the moment each of us suffered loss—we had our eyes fixed on the legacy God wants to bring from that loss? What if, at the point of acknowledging our longings, we looked for the ways God would use that for good in our lives, as well as in the lives of others?

If you and I kept our eyes fixed forward, rather than downward on our disappointments, perhaps we wouldn't miss the ways God is already using our pain to produce something lasting in us and in others.

Ellen, whose story I told you in chapter 9, has legitimate concerns about dying and leaving her teenage daughter to go through womanhood without a mother. And yet Ellen says, "God has changed my prayer from giving me additional years of life to dying well. I want my loved ones to see the reality of God in my life no matter what the journey may be. I want to die well to inspire others to live well and to love God well."

And Ellen's legacy is already being lived out. Her daughter recently told her, "Mom, I hope when I get close to death, I will handle it like you do."

"That made me feel that it's all worthwhile," Ellen said.

Trusting in the Dark

We all live with the hopes that our tears will someday be worthwhile. Alejandra was able to see it in just one piece of encouragement to the friend of a friend. Ellen is beginning to see it in how her daughter has reacted to her illness. But it's difficult when you and I can't see it yet. That is where our trust comes in.

Look back with me at some of the women you've met in this book who have had to trust God in the dark and yet are now beginning to see God work a legacy through their lives, and in some cases, the lives of those they love.

A Legacy of Trust

Lissa, the young bride from chapter 1 who was abandoned early in her marriage (and her pregnancy), could only see uncertainty and financial hardships ahead of her. But God saw a young woman who was willing to surrender her son to God, just like Hannah was. Lissa's story is far from over. God is just beginning to do something in her and her little Samuel's life.

I received an email from Lissa just yesterday, along with a picture of her and her son. In her email she said, "Samuel is now a month old, and I have heard nothing from my husband. But God has been ever so faithful to us both and I feel more blessed then I have ever felt in my entire life.

"I was having my quiet time this morning and was praying, asking God why my husband hasn't showed up, why he hasn't called, and God gave me exactly what I needed to be assured of His control—that right now He is protecting Samuel and me, and that I need to rely on Him and focus on raising Samuel for the Lord. Everything else will fall into place in the way and timing that God determines."

What surrender! What a legacy this little boy will have with a mom who knows now, at the beginning of his little life, that God is on the throne and in control of everything.

A Legacy of Faith

Alena (from chapter 2) , who saw cancer take her husband's life and who has since surrendered to the Lord her own brain tumor, often thinks of what she will leave behind as a legacy and testimony to her faith.

"I want my family and my children to see God written all over my life," she said. "I want them to know that through it all, God can steady you and hold you, no matter what comes your way. They do know that. But I want them to see in me how God did exactly that so they know that there *is* a God and He is the Sustainer, and He is hope, and He is the giver of strength."

A Legacy of Grace

Gayla, from chapter 4, who lost one beloved woman in her life after another—all in the span of a few years—gained a tender heart and an ability to minister to others far more effectively now that she's walked through the valley of brokenness.

And Krissy, who struggled with her husband's addiction to pornography, learned through her situation that "all have sinned and fall short of the glory of God" (Romans 3:23 NASB) and now has a better understanding of God's grace and forgiveness to all of us. She and her husband have also seen God strengthen their bond with each other because they were honest with one another and have had to rely on God to see their marriage through.

A Legacy of Compassion

When God took Amanda's husband on a spring day as he was working at the church (chapter 5), that incident looked almost cruel and calculating. But God was still over it all and apparently wanted to impact an entire church, draw a pastor's wife into deeper intimacy with Himself, and cause a little girl named Belle to have a compassion few children her age can demonstrate.

When I recently asked Amanda what kinds of blessings have come from her situation, she talked of her daughter's sensitivity and kindness toward others—something she believes Belle gained through the loss of her father.

"I see a child who, at three-and-a-half years of age, is able to meet people at their emotional level. A couple of people in our church have had parents die—how sweet that one person in particular was able to talk to Belle about this. Belle looked at Laurie and said, 'Laurie, you miss your daddy, don't you?' Laurie said, 'Yes, Belle, I do.' Belle then said, 'Laurie, it's okay to cry. It's okay to be sad. It's okay to miss your daddy.'

"It's amazing to see such a young child express very eloquently and clearly what she's thinking. I believe one of the legacies coming out of this is the passion that Belle has for people—for their emotional state and knowing where they are. She gives a hug where she senses it is needed and smiles when she sees that someone needs encouragement.

"I know she is going to be a force to be reckoned with. A perfect combination of love and determination. I want to cultivate that and let her grow into the woman of God that He created her to be."

A Legacy of Serving Others

Katherine, from chapter 8, who lost her son to alleged suicide, says, "Obviously God won't be giving my son back to me, but He reassures me that I will see Donald in heaven one day. I feel like He has a plan for me in all of this, although I am not sure what it is. It may be to help other parents who suffer from the loss of a child. If it is determined that my son really did commit suicide, which I am trying to accept, it may be that I can help other survivors of suicide.

"The small things we do every day of our lives, in interacting with other people, in sharing God's Word and living a testimony, is making a difference in people's lives and we don't really even know it," Katherine said. She saw that to be the case in her son's life when more than 500 people attended his memorial service and many of them told her of how he had influenced their lives. "Donald made a difference in a lot of people's lives. His death has actually changed the lives of quite a few young men he was friends with at his university." And now she is seeing how *her* life, through his death, can positively change the lives of others too.

A Legacy of Teaching

In chapter 9, we looked at Pam's experiences, which have helped shape her faith, including her round-the-clock care for her youngest daughter, Naomi, who suffered brain damage in a car accident when she was just 17.

"God has grown my faith over the years and my heart was full of wonderful lessons to share with people, yet I didn't have any confidence to get up in a class and teach or speak. I wanted to be used of the Lord so desperately, but didn't know how to share with others. God opened the door of ministry for me after Naomi's accident through Caring Bridge [an Internet site in which she can post updates on Naomi, as well as her thoughts, prayers, and reflections on what God is doing through her in all of this]. He took all that was in my heart and mind and allowed it to flow to the pages of the Caring Bridge journals. What I couldn't do outwardly with my mouth I was able to do through written words. I thank the Lord Jesus and praise Him for the way He has used me for His glory over the last four years. Life is still hard, with my daughter still in need of 24-hour care; but I can see God's hand continually using my life and my daughter's life to help others grow in their faith."

Pam excitedly told me about her latest ministry project with Naomi. "I just finished a tract with some of Nay's and my stories. We printed some copies last night and Naomi was so excited to hand out about thirty tonight for Halloween. Praise the Lord! He has blessed us with a great opportunity to share His Word."

God Knew You Could Handle It

When God asked for Abraham's willingness to be obedient to Him, even to the point of sacrificing his only son, God already knew that Abraham would pass the test.

> God will carry you through whatever He asks of you.

Whatever you have lost up to this point, whatever you feel you are losing now, God saw this day ahead of time. And my friend, He didn't allow it to *see* if you would be surrendered and obedient to Him. He allowed it because He *knew* you would eventually surrender it to Him. He is mindful of you, that you are but dust. And He will carry you through whatever He asks of you. He saw that *you* would be able to get through this with Him. He knew the tears would come. But He also knows what's necessary for developing you into the woman He wants to build a legacy upon.

I'm sure Hannah, whose life story we have followed throughout this book, didn't think in terms of a legacy when she was dealing with the disappointment and frustration of trying to have a child. She quite possibly only saw her tears, her lack, her heartache. But God took this barren woman who was willing to surrender her long-awaited son to God and built a legacy through both her *and* her son.

One Last Look at Hannah

Hopefully by now you feel a kindred spirit with Hannah, this woman whose tears you have traced and whose hurt you have related to as you've seen her cry out to God, finally receive what she wanted, and then give it back to God and trust Him all her days. God honored Hannah's trust. We saw in the last chapter how Samuel grew in stature and in favor with God and men—even within that reckless, ungodly house of Eli—in the same ways that Jesus, the Son of God, grew and matured. Does that convince you that God takes care of what we commit to Him in a far better way than we could take care of it ourselves? Perhaps by sharing a household with Peninnah's other children (and who knows how obstinate they might have been), Samuel might never have known the dedication and reverence to God that he grew to know when he was in some ways, alone, in the house of Eli.

We see Samuel's legacy in this story, and with it, Hannah's too. One Bible commentator says this:

> Samuel grew up to become the last judge, an outstanding and gifted prophet, and the one who would anoint the first two kings of Israel. Samuel was a pivotal spiritual leader who turned the nation toward Yahweh. His mother Hannah played her part in this spiritual awakening as she trusted God, leaving for all posterity an example of determined devotion in her motherhood.[1]

Don't underestimate the legacy Hannah left simply by raising her child—in his first few years—to honor and obey God.

The *Women's Study Bible* says, "Though leadership that reverenced and obeyed God was practically non-existent at that time in Israel's history, both reverence and obedience to God were modeled by Hannah for her son Samuel, who in turn modeled them for a nation. The example of Samuel's life also was observed by Israel's first two kings."[2]

Through Hannah's *personal devotion* to God, her son became one of Israel's greatest prophets, who anointed Israel's greatest king. And Hannah's *obedience* to God resulted in not only a legacy for a nation, but for her as well. I can't help but think that Hannah's personal relationship with God—her understanding that He saw her tears, that He remembered her, and that He came through for her in a strong and mighty way—was how she could pass a legacy to her son of revering and honoring God. And yet had Hannah not suffered loss in her life (through her years of longing for a child and being harassed in the process), she clearly would not have become the legacy she and her son are today.

Hannah's legacy is also seen through her song of praise to God (which we saw in chapter 9) in the wake of giving up her child. Do you realize that song is similar to the one that Mary of Nazareth sang centuries later, in the presence of her relative, Elizabeth, shortly after being told she would bear the long-awaited Messiah (Luke 1:46-55)? Scholars believe Mary's jubilant song of praise to God (which we now call the Magnificat) was modeled after Hannah's prayer.[3] That tells me that if a young Jewish girl could quote Hannah's prayer in her moment of overwhelming praise, that many others throughout history probably knew and even repeated her song. Imagine that! Throughout history, they knew of Hannah's story, and they knew of her praise in spite of her sacrifice—even before it became included in what we now know as the Bible.

As we saw in chapter 9, Scripture says Hannah was blessed with five more children. And most importantly, her story of faith, pouring her heart out to God, sacrifice, and follow-through is recorded in the Scriptures. God chose *her* story to help tell *His* story.

I want my story to help tell His story as well. I know you want that too. The key is obedience, surrender, and continued trust.

Have you ever thought about the generations to come who will be affected by your obedience to God today? Or by your disobedience or failure to surrender your all to God? The risk of the latter isn't worth it. God knows how to steer our lives in an eternally good way. So let Him have His way with you.

Influencing the Next Generation

We just read about how Amanda's little daughter, Belle, is beginning to show a compassion and understanding of others as a result of what she and her mother have been through.

Let's look now at how Ellen's teenage daughter, Mary, reacted to her mom's cancer and how God is developing in her an intimacy with Him that she hadn't known before:

"My first reaction to the news that my mom had terminal cancer was, *How is a 15-year-old supposed to respond to this?* All I could think was, *Don't cry, Mary, don't cry. They don't need to see you cry!* Well, that lasted for about ten seconds. I broke down and cried. My mom rubbed my back and told me it was all right to cry and that they understand if I was mad at God. *Mad at God?* I thought. *Why would I be mad at God?* Sure, I was confused as to why God would allow such a committed Christian woman to get cancer, but I wasn't mad at God. I knew He had a plan and He was in control. For that I was very grateful, because I had no idea what to do.

"That was probably the hardest part for me, not being able to make my mom better. I have seen her too weak from chemo to make dinner or help my dad with something. I have seen my mom bedridden because of a tiny cold. I have seen her in the hospital for two weeks and forced to wear a protective helmet because her platelet count was so low, and have to wear a mask because the stem-cell transplant lowered her white and red blood cell count so much that it left her defenseless against germs. Through all of this I realized there was one thing I could do for my mom that no one else could do quite like I could—I could make her laugh. My mom absolutely loves corny stuff (for what reason, I do not know). So, as soon as I realized how I could bless my mom, I became the queen of corny jokes. My goal for the day, every day, was to make my mom smile.

I didn't care if I had a bad day at school or was tired or was in a bad mood. All of that seems pretty unimportant when your mom has cancer. [Mary even helped her mom laugh during what she calls her 'worst memory' of helping her mom shave her head once her hair began falling out.]

"If you had told me a month before my mom's diagnosis what my life was going to be like for that next year and a half, I would not have believed you. I could never imagine my mom getting cancer and I could never imagine having to handle everything that I did. But that's the point, isn't it? I *couldn't* handle it, and I didn't handle it. God did. Over that year and a half my faith grew so much. Hearing from God [through the Scriptures and through her circumstances] became a daily thing for me. I knew that He was with me, guiding me, giving me the emotional and physical energy to do everything I needed to. I was and am able to trust in Him and know that He has it all under control.

"God is good. He always has been, and He always will be."

"If there is one thing I can say through this whole thing, it is that God is good. He always has been, and He always will be. I now know why God has given my mom cancer. So she can tell others her story. Would she be in this book if this hadn't happened? No. Would she be able to talk to hundreds of people about God and how amazing He is and how much He has blessed her through cancer? He has given my mom a very personal, heart-wrenching story that is pretty hard to ignore."

There it is again. God is able to tell *His* story through Ellen's story. And God is able to tell His story through Mary's telling of her mother's story. God is leaving a legacy through our tears, through our words, and through our declaration that, in spite of the loss, He is God and He is good.

When You Can't See It

Maybe by now you're thinking, *But I can't see how God is building a legacy out of my loss right now. All I can see is the pain.*

That's all right if you can't see it. In fact, God doesn't need you to see or understand or even approve for Him to do the work He wants to do. He will do it regardless. And if He decides it's good for you to see it, you will.

Sometimes, in God's grace, He allows us to see the impact we've had on another person's life. And that is an exciting thing when it happens. Yet I'm sure there are many more instances in which God doesn't necessarily let us see what He is doing. Maybe that will be one of our surprises when we finally get to heaven—to see what He did in the spiritual realm with something as small as a kindness you showed to someone when you weren't feeling well, or something as big as a loss you endured that helped you, or another person—or countless others—understand who God is. God can take anything you give Him and work wonders through it and sometimes, just sometimes, He actually blesses you with the realization that you had a small part in it. God isn't obligated to give us credit. (Mainly because He knows it is His Son's work in us that enables us to do the very thing that caused another's heart to change.) But He does reward those who seek Him. And I have a feeling that is one of the sweet ways He rewards us—by letting us know, every once in a while, that our obedience to Him made a difference in someone's life.

Turning Loss into Legacy

I could go on and on with the stories of how God turned a loss—or a longing—into a legacy. But I have a feeling the next story that needs to be told is yours.

So before you close this book, I want to remind you how you can put yourself in a position to allow God to turn your longings—and losses—into a legacy.

Cultivate a Life of Prayer

"Prayer does not equip us for greater works—prayer *is* the greater work…We do not pray to receive from God, we pray to get to know God. As we spend time in His presence through prayer He changes us. He makes us more like Him. He unites our hearts with His. There is no better bonding than the bonding we do with God's heart in prayer."[4]

As you spend time in God's presence, He will lay on your heart how to pray, what to watch for, and where He wants you. As He reveals this to you, He is directing you toward fulfilling the legacy He has already written with your life.

Consider Your Life His

When you realize you have no rights of your own and that all of you belongs to God, you will hold whatever you have with open hands…and God will not have to pry your fingers open. Come to Him daily with palms open, willing to give Him what He asks, willing to receive from Him what He gives.

Commit Your Life to Him Daily

A legacy doesn't happen overnight. Nor does it suddenly arrive in our life as we step into God's grand plan. Legacies are built moment by moment, bit by bit, day by day as we make decision after decision. Will each decision you make be based on His will or yours? That, my friend, will determine the nature of your legacy.

One Day at a Time

Michele, whose story of "pouring out in prayer" opened chapter 4, told me of what happened just after she recommitted her heart and life to Christ. She went from the high of knowing God and His grace to the low of being reminded that she lives in a world that sometimes downright stinks!

Listen to her honest words shortly after writing me about what

God was beginning to do in her life, and see if you can detect the legacy God is already building in her:

"I was put to the test after I recommitted myself. Someone stole our cherry tree last night from our front yard. My son planted this tree last week. It was sweet-looking and represented to me a new beginning. Around 11:00 last night we heard a noise like our garage door was trying to be opened. It woke us up, but I was too tired to go check and even told my son it sounded like our neighbor's garage door. We then fell peacefully back to sleep. *What would I do if I caught someone, anyhow? Nothing I have is worth getting hurt or killed over.* As soon as my neighbor texted me this morning, saying, 'Your tree is gone!!!' I knew it was a test of how I was going to react. I went to the window and looked, and yes, the tree was gone. I went outside and asked a neighbor if he saw anything, and then said, 'It's sad, but I'll pray for whoever did it.'

"A PVC pipe that had been pounded deep into the dirt to hold the tree steady and feed it was also gone. The thieves took the tree, the soil around its roots, *and* the PVC pipe and left a trail of dirt to the street gutter two houses down! Anyhow, as I drove my son to his school, my son and I prayed for that person or persons. 'I'm not mad,' I told him. But we were both sad over his work lost in this and the loss of our forty-dollar tree. We were perplexed that someone would risk going to jail over stealing such a minor thing. We had wanted a tree in our front yard for nine years and had finally gotten one after a fun day of tree shopping. At least the thieves could not get into our garage, and nothing else was stolen.

"The incident rocked my peace momentarily. I was tired and frustrated over the fact a thief had been that close to my front door and my son's room as we slept. As I've wondered about what to do, I've decided we will plant another tree in the same spot next month.

"The Bible says if someone asks for your shirt, give him your jacket too (Matthew 5:40). So maybe I'll plant another fruit tree, this one even bigger, and leave a note tied onto it that says, 'You obviously need it more than I do, so God bless you with the fruit it produces.' Of course, my flesh wants to add a line that says, 'And by the way, you broke our hearts when you stole our cherry tree; but we forgive you, again. But please don't come back!'"

Michele admitted, "This kind of thing is a test, and I'm going to pass it with a smile on my face because I accept that we live in a fallen world; and people, places, and things will let me down, but my serenity will not be stolen! The tree is gone, but it is still going to produce fruit in me—the fruit of the Spirit, that is."

Michele's reaction to her stolen cherry tree showed more about who she is in Christ than she realized. She showed her son (and her Facebook friends with whom she shared this story) that her treasure is now in heaven—not "on earth where moth and rust destroy"[5] nor in her yard—"where thieves break in and steal."

Your Moment by Moment

What is happening in your life from day to day to test your strength, to shape your character, and to remind you that you are not in control, and that this world is not the extent of your hopes? Your legacy—a faith and trust in God no matter what—is being built moment by moment, day by day, as you depend on Him in your disappointments, look to Him in your losses, and trust Him with your tears.

We want to be living "at such a level of human dependence upon Jesus Christ that His life is being exhibited moment by moment in us."[6]

> There is no such thing as an accident or a disaster because God is in control of all things.

Can God depend on *your* trust today even if there are no leads, nothing to look forward to, no signs of His abundant blessing, and you wake up to a hole in the center of your front yard? When you have that kind of trust, my friend, you are *already* living a legacy.

As you sit with this book in your hands

and reflect on your life, things may appear disappointing compared to what you had imagined, compared to what you had hoped for, compared to what someone had promised you. But again, God knows exactly what He's doing. There is no such thing as an accident or a disaster because God is in control of all things.

Won't you trust Him with the purposes He has for *your* life? He is shaping you into His masterpiece (Ephesians 2:10). Your disaster or disappointment didn't take Him by surprise. In His all-knowing, all-loving goodness, He determined that you would follow Him in spite of that...for some unexplainable reason known only to Him. For some unfathomable glory reserved only for Him. And for some unimaginable joy that will someday be yours.

Turning Your Loss into a Legacy

It's time to make what you have read about in this book real in your life. Prayerfully consider the following steps and give some thought to how you will apply them to your life so you can start building your legacy today:

Cultivate a Life of Prayer

What does your prayer life look like right now? Do you need to be more disciplined so you don't miss what God is wanting to show you and reveal to you about Himself? Consider starting a prayer journal in which you record what you are praying for. It's a good exercise to write down your prayer requests and record when and how God answers them. That will help keep you in a "dialogue" with God and also remind you of the times He does answer.

Consider Your Life His

Are there some longings in your heart that you are still holding onto rather than laying them on the altar in surrender to Him? Are there aspects of your personality you don't necessarily want Him to change, or certain "rights" you are insisting on, or certain grievances you are refusing to release? When you come to God and say, "Lord, all that I am and all that I have is Yours to do with as You please," you will experience His peace and start living the way He desires.

Commit Your Life to Him Daily

Commitment to Christ *should* be a one-time thing. But we often mess up, don't we? Or we let our pain and frustration get the better of us. In my life, to commit myself to Him daily involves saying to Him every morning as I rise from bed, "God, please take Your rightful place on the throne of my life so that every longing I experience, every decision I make, every word I say, and every thought I have is *Yours*." Highlight that prayer or write one of your own that you will say daily to Him and mean it with all of your heart.

A Prayer for Finishing Well

Father God and Giver of Every Perfect Gift:

You have given me "gifts" that I have not necessarily wanted in my life. But I understand now that everything You have allowed in my life is to ultimately bring You glory. I want to be remembered as one who lived well, and I also want to experience Your joy as I surrender to Your will for my life rather than my own. Thank You for giving me the privilege of being a part of Your plan to let others know who You are. Help me to never forget that You have seen my tears, You know my past, and You are continuing to write my story—which is ultimately *Your* story—so that You can be glorified now and forevermore.

Appendices

How to Know You Are God's Child

Although we are all God's *creation*, we are not all God's *children*. Scripture says each of us is a sinner from the time we are born (Psalm 51:5) and we are all, naturally, children of Satan, who is the father of lies (John 8:44). But God has provided a way for us to become adopted by Him and become His own (Romans 8:14-17).

To be cleansed of your sin and receive salvation in Christ (and therefore be considered God's child) you must be in a relationship with Jesus Christ, God's Son, the only bridge that can close the gap between your sin and a holy God. A relationship with God, and that cleansing, begins when you surrender your heart to Him:

1. Admit you are a sinner by nature and there is nothing you can do on your own to make up for that sin in the eyes of a holy God (Romans 3:23).

2. Accept the sacrifice that God provided—the death of His righteous and sinless Son, Jesus, on the cross on your behalf—in order to bring you into communion with Him.

3. Enter into a love relationship with God, through Jesus, as a response to His love and forgiveness toward you. (For more on developing and maintaining an intimate relationship with God, see my book *Letting God Meet Your Emotional Needs* [Harvest House Publishers], available at www.StrengthForTheSoul.com.)

4. Surrender to God your right to yourself and acknowledge His right to carry out His plans for you and to mold you, shape you, and transform you for His pleasure.

5. Find a pastor or women's ministry director at a Bible-teaching church in your area or a trusted Christian friend and tell him or her of your decision to surrender your life to Christ. They will want to pray for you and get you the support and resources you need to grow in your new relationship with Jesus.

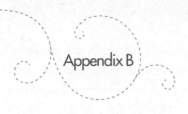

Comfort & Promises for Hurting Hearts

All Scripture passages are in the New King James Version, unless otherwise indicated.

When You're Searching for a Reason for Your Pain

"My thoughts are not your thoughts,
  nor are your ways My ways," says the Lord.
"For as the heavens are higher than the earth,
  so are My ways higher than your ways,
  and My thoughts than your thoughts" (Isaiah 55:8-9).

The Lord gave another message to Jeremiah. He said, "Go down to the potter's shop, and I will speak to you there." So I did as he told me and found the potter working at his wheel. But the jar he was making did not turn out as he had hoped, so he crushed it into a lump of clay and started over.

Then the Lord gave me this message: "O Israel, can I not do to you as this potter has done to his clay? As the clay is in the potter's hand, so are you in my hand" (Jeremiah 18:1-6 NLT).

We know that all things work together for good to those who love God, to those who are the called according to His purpose. For whom He foreknew, He also predestined to be conformed to the image of His Son (Romans 8:28-29).

Blessed be the God and Father of our Lord Jesus Christ, the Father of mercies and God of all comfort, who comforts us in all our tribulation, that we may be able to comfort those who are in any trouble, with the comfort with which we ourselves are comforted by God (2 Corinthians 1:3-4).

Our light affliction, which is but for a moment, is working for us a far more exceeding and eternal weight of glory, while we do not look at the things which are seen, but at the things which are not seen. For the things which are seen are temporary, but the things which are not seen are eternal (2 Corinthians 4:17-18).

My brethren, count it all joy when you fall into various trials, knowing that the testing of your faith produces patience. But let patience have its perfect work, that you may be perfect and complete, lacking nothing (James 1:2-4).

When You're Struggling with Guilt or Shame

I acknowledged my sin to You,
And my iniquity I have not hidden.
I said, "I will confess my transgressions to the LORD,"
And You forgave the iniquity of my sin (Psalm 32:5).

Have mercy upon me, O God,
According to Your lovingkindness;
According to the multitude of Your tender mercies,
Blot out my transgressions.
Wash me thoroughly from my iniquity,
And cleanse me from my sin (Psalm 51:1-2).

You, Lord, are good, and ready to forgive,
And abundant in mercy to all those who call upon You (Psalm 86:5).

As far as the east is from the west,
So far has He removed our transgressions from us (Psalm 103:12).

Search me, O God, and know my heart;
Try me, and know my anxieties;
And see if there is any wicked way in me,
And lead me in the way everlasting (Psalm 139:23-24).

I, even I, am He who blots out your transgressions for My own sake;
And I will not remember your sins (Isaiah 43:25).

I will forgive their iniquity, and their sin I will remember no more (Jeremiah 31:34).

He will again have compassion on us;
And subdue our iniquities.
You will cast all our sins
Into the depths of the sea (Micah 7:19).

There is therefore now no condemnation to those who are in Christ Jesus, who do not walk according to the flesh, but according to the Spirit. For the law of the Spirit of life in Christ Jesus has made me free from the law of sin and death (Romans 8:1-2).

If we confess our sins, He is faithful and just to forgive us our sins and to cleanse us from all unrighteousness (1 John 1:9).

In Him we have redemption through His blood, the forgiveness of sins, according to the riches of His grace (Ephesians 1:7).

When You Need God's Comfort and Deliverance

Is anything too hard for the LORD? (Genesis 18:14).

Be strong and of good courage, do not fear nor be afraid of them; for the LORD your God, He is the One who goes with you. He will not leave you nor forsake you (Deuteronomy 31:6).

I will both lie down in peace, and sleep;
For You alone, O LORD, make me dwell in safety (Psalm 4:8).

His anger is but for a moment,
His favor is for life;
Weeping may endure for a night,
But joy comes in the morning (Psalm 30:5).

You are my hiding place;
You shall preserve me from trouble;
You shall surround me with songs of deliverance (Psalm 32:7).

Many are the afflictions of the righteous,
But the LORD delivers him out of them all (Psalm 34:19).

I waited patiently for the LORD;
And He inclined to me,
And heard my cry.
He also brought me up out of a horrible pit,
Out of the miry clay,
And set my feet upon a rock,
And established my steps.
He has put a new song in my mouth—
Praise to our God;
Many will see it and fear,
And will trust in the LORD (Psalm 40:1-3).

God is our refuge and strength,
A very present help in trouble.
Therefore we will not fear,
Even though the earth be removed,
And though the mountains be carried into the midst of the sea;
Though its waters roar and be troubled,
Though the mountains shake with its swelling (Psalm 46:1-3).

You have been a shelter for me,
A strong tower from the enemy (Psalm 61:3).

Trust in Him at all times, you people;
Pour out your heart before Him;
God is a refuge for us (Psalm 62:8).

Whoever dwells in the shelter of the Most High
    will rest in the shadow of the Almighty.
I will say of the LORD, "He is my refuge and my fortress,
    my God, in whom I trust" (Psalm 91:1-2 NIV).

Great peace have those who love Your law,
    and nothing causes them to stumble (Psalm 119:165).

My help comes from the LORD,
Who made heaven and earth.
He will not allow your foot to be moved;
He who keeps you will not slumber (Psalm 121:2-3).

Where can I go from Your Spirit?
Or where can I flee from Your presence?
If I ascend into heaven, You are there;
If I make my bed in hell, behold, You are there.
If I take the wings of the morning,
And dwell in the uttermost parts of the sea,
Even there Your hand shall lead me,

And Your right hand shall hold me.
If I say, "Surely the darkness shall fall on me,"
Even the night shall be light about me;
Indeed, the darkness shall not hide from You,
But the night shines as the day;
The darkness and the light are both alike to You (Psalm 139:7-12).

The LORD is gracious and full of compassion,
Slow to anger and great in mercy.
The LORD is good to all,
And His tender mercies are over all His works (Psalm 145:8-9).

Fear not, for I am with you;
Be not dismayed, for I am your God.
I will strengthen you,
Yes, I will help you,
I will uphold you with My righteous right hand (Isaiah 41:10).

When you pass through the waters, I will be with you;
And through the rivers, they shall not overflow you.
When you walk through the fire, you shall not be burned,
Nor shall the flame scorch you (Isaiah 43:2).

The mountains shall depart
And the hills be removed,
But My kindness shall not depart from you,
Nor shall My covenant of peace be removed (Isaiah 54:10).

"No weapon forged against you will prevail, and you will refute every
tongue that accuses you. This is the heritage of the servants of the
LORD, and this is their vindication from me," declares the LORD (Isaiah 54:17 NIV).

The LORD has appeared of old to me, saying:
"Yes, I have loved you with an everlasting love;
Therefore with lovingkindness I have drawn you" (Jeremiah 31:3).

The LORD is good,
A stronghold in the day of trouble;
And He knows those who trust in Him (Nahum 1:7).

What then shall we say to these things? If God is for us, who can be against us? (Romans 8:31).

I am convinced that nothing can ever separate us from God's love. Neither death nor life, neither angels nor demons, neither our fears for today nor our worries about tomorrow—not even the powers of hell can separate us from God's love. No power in the sky above or in the earth below—indeed, nothing in all creation will ever be able to separate us from the love of God that is revealed in Christ Jesus our Lord (Romans 8:38-39 NLT).

Blessed be the God and Father of our Lord Jesus Christ, the Father of mercies and God of all comfort, who comforts us in all our tribulation, that we may be able to comfort those who are in any trouble, with the comfort with which we ourselves are comforted by God (2 Corinthians 1:3-4).

He Himself has said, "I will never leave you nor forsake you" (Hebrews 13:5).

When You Need God's Comfort in the Face of Death

Even though I walk through the valley of the shadow of death,
    I will fear no evil,
for you are with me;
    your rod and your staff,
    they comfort me (Psalm 23:4 ESV).

Precious in the sight of the LORD
Is the death of His saints (Psalm 116:15).

The LORD cares deeply
> when his loved ones die (Psalm 116:15 NLT).

Jesus said to her, "I am the resurrection and the life. He who believes in Me, though he may die, he shall live. And whoever lives and believes in Me shall never die" (John 11:25-26).

If I go and prepare a place for you, I will come again and receive you to Myself; that where I am, there you may be also (John 14:3).

When You Need Hope

The young lions lack and suffer hunger;
But those who seek the LORD shall not lack any good thing (Psalm 34:10).

Delight yourself also in the LORD,
And He shall give you the desires of your heart (Psalm 37:4).

The LORD God is a sun and shield;
The LORD will give grace and glory;
No good thing will He withhold
From those who walk uprightly (Psalm 84:11).

The LORD upholds all who fall,
And raises up all who are bowed down.
> The eyes of all look expectantly to You,
And You give them their food in due season.
> You open Your hand
And satisfy the desire of every living thing (Psalm 145:14-16).

Those who wait on the LORD
Shall renew their strength;
They shall mount up with wings like eagles,

They shall run and not be weary,
They shall walk and not faint (Isaiah 40:31).

"I know the thoughts that I think toward you," says the LORD, "thoughts of peace and not of evil, to give you a future and a hope" (Jeremiah 29:11).

In all these things we are more than conquerors through Him who loved us (Romans 8:37).

My God shall supply all your need according to His riches in glory by Christ Jesus (Philippians 4:19).

You are of God, little children, and have overcome them, because He who is in you is greater than he who is in the world (1 John 4:4).

When You Need Healing

He heals the brokenhearted
And binds up their wounds (Psalm 147:3).

Surely He has borne our griefs
And carried our sorrows;
Yet we esteemed Him stricken,
Smitten by God, and afflicted.
But He was wounded for our transgressions,
He was bruised for our iniquities;
The chastisement for our peace was upon Him,
And by His stripes we are healed (Isaiah 53:4-5).

The Spirit of the LORD is upon Me,
Because He has anointed Me
To preach the gospel to the poor;
He has sent Me to heal the brokenhearted,

To proclaim liberty to the captives
And recovery of sight to the blind
To set at liberty those who are oppressed (Luke 4:18).

When You Need a New Start

Create in me a clean heart, O God,
And renew a steadfast spirit within me.
Do not cast me away from Your presence,
And do not take Your Holy Spirit from me.
Restore to me the joy of Your salvation,
And uphold me by Your generous Spirit (Psalm 51:10-12).

I will give you a new heart and put a new spirit within you; I will take the heart of stone out of your flesh and give you a heart of flesh (Ezekiel 36:26).

Anyone who belongs to Christ has become a new person. The old life is gone; a new life has begun! (2 Corinthians 5:17 NLT).

I have been crucified with Christ; it is no longer I who live, but Christ lives in me; and the life which I now live in the flesh I live by faith in the Son of God, who loved me and gave Himself for me (Galatians 2:20).

When You Need a Reminder That He Sees You

You number my wanderings;
Put my tears into Your bottle;
Are they not in Your book? (Psalm 56:8).

You formed my inward parts;
You covered me in my mother's womb.
I will praise You, for I am fearfully and wonderfully made;
Marvelous are Your works,
And that my soul knows very well.
My frame was not hidden from You,
When I was made in secret,
And skillfully wrought in the lowest parts of the earth.
Your eyes saw my substance, being yet unformed.
And in Your book they all were written,
The days fashioned for me,
When as yet there were none of them.
How precious also are Your thoughts to me, O God!
How great is the sum of them!
If I should count them, they would be more in number than the
sand;
When I awake, I am still with You (Psalm 139:13-18).

Can a woman forget her nursing child,
And not have compassion on the son of her womb?
Surely they may forget,
Yet I will not forget you.
See, I have inscribed you on the palms of My hands;
Your walls are continually before Me (Isaiah 49:15-16).

Are not two sparrows sold for a copper coin? And not one of them
falls to the ground apart from your Father's will. But the very hairs of
your head are all numbered. Do not fear therefore; you are of more
value than many sparrows (Matthew 10:29-31).

The eyes of the LORD are on the righteous,
And His ears are open to their prayers;
But the face of the LORD is against those who do evil (1 Peter 3:12).

When You Need Spiritual Strength

The weapons we fight with are not the weapons of the world. On the contrary, they have divine power to demolish strongholds. We demolish arguments and every pretension that sets itself up against the knowledge of God, and we take captive every thought to make it obedient to Christ (2 Corinthians 10:4-5 NIV).

Now to Him who is able to do exceedingly abundantly above all that we ask or think, according to the power that works in us (Ephesians 3:20).

Be strong in the Lord and in the power of His might. Put on the whole armor of God, that you may be able to stand against the wiles of the devil. For we do not wrestle against flesh and blood, but against principalities, against powers, against the rulers of the darkness of this age, against spiritual hosts of wickedness in the heavenly places. Therefore take up the whole armor of God, that you may be able to withstand in the evil day, and having done all, to stand.

Stand therefore, having girded your waist with truth, having put on the breastplate of righteousness, and having shod your feet with the preparation of the gospel of peace; above all, taking the shield of faith with which you will be able to quench all the fiery darts of the wicked one. And take the helmet of salvation, and the sword of the Spirit, which is the word of God; praying always with all prayer and supplication in the Spirit, being watchful to this end with all perseverance and supplication for all the saints (Ephesians 6:10-18).

Be anxious for nothing, but in everything by prayer and supplication, with thanksgiving, let your requests be made known to God; and the peace of God, which surpasses all understanding, will guard your hearts and minds through Christ Jesus (Philippians 4:6-7).

Whatever is true, whatever is noble, whatever is right, whatever is pure, whatever is lovely whatever is admirable—if anything is excellent or praiseworthy—think about such things (Philippians 4:8 NIV).

I can do all things through Christ who strengthens me (Philippians 4:13).

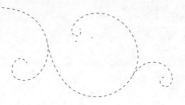

Notes

Chapter 1—The Missing Piece

1. For more on this concept, see my book *Letting God Meet Your Emotional Needs* (Eugene, OR: Harvest House Publishers). It is available at my website: www.StrengthForTheSoul.com.

2. Circumstances that allowed for polygamy under Jewish law included the situation in which a woman's husband died and her husband's brother was allowed to take her as a wife, if he desired, so she would be provided for. Scripture isn't clear if this was the reason Elkanah had two wives, but we can probably assume this because Elkanah was a God-fearing man who honored the yearly sacrifices under the Jewish law.

3. Isaiah 54:5 says, "Your husband is your Maker, Whose name is the LORD of hosts; and your Redeemer is the Holy One of Israel, who is called the God of all the earth" (NASB).

Chapter 2—The Provocation

1. *The Nelson Study Bible*, New King James Version (Nashville, TN: Thomas Nelson Publishers, 1997), p. 1208.

Chapter 4—Pouring It Out

1. The Hebrew term *mar*, translated "bitter," can also mean angry, or chafed. E-Sword, Strong's Hebrew and Greek Dictionaries.

2. The Message, which is written in everyday, idiomatic English, representing the way people think and talk today.

3. *The Woman's Study Bible* (Nashville, TN: Thomas Nelson Publishers, 1995), p. 445.

4. *The Woman's Study Bible*, p. 445.

Chapter 5—Sudden Backfire

1. Cindi McMenamin, *When Women Walk Alone* (Eugene, OR: Harvest House Publishers, 2002, 2012). This book is available at www.StrengthForTheSoul.com or anywhere you purchase books.

2. *The Reformation Study Bible* (Orlando: Ligonier Ministries/P&R Publishing Company, 2005), p. 378.

Chapter 6—Affirmation

1. Romans 8:28.

2. Oswald Chambers, *My Utmost for His Highest* (Grand Rapids, MI: Discovery House Publishers, 1992), January 25.

Chapter 7—The Arrival

1. Henry T. Blackaby and Claude V. King, *Experiencing God: Knowing and Doing the Will of God* (Nashville, TN: Lifeway Press, 1990), p. 89.

Chapter 8—The Ultimate Sacrifice

1. In Matthew 17:19-20, Jesus' disciples asked Him why they couldn't drive out a demon from a demon-possessed man. Jesus replied, "Because you have so little faith. Truly I tell you, if you have faith as small as a mustard seed, you can say to this mountain, 'Move from here to there,' and it will move. Nothing will be impossible for you."

2. *The Women's Study Bible* (Nashville, TN: Thomas Nelson Publishing, 1995), p. 445.

3. *The Women's Study Bible*, p. 446.

4. Oswald Chambers, *My Utmost for His Highest* (Grand Rapids, MI: Discovery House Publishers, 1992), October 31.

5. Chambers, August 14.

6. Chambers, July 16.

7. Chambers, October 31.

Chapter 9—Continuing On

1. New King James Version.

Chapter 10—Looking Ahead

1. *The Women's Study Bible* (Nashville, TN: Thomas Nelson Publishing, 1995), p. 445.

2. *The Women's Study Bible*, p. 446.

3. *The Reformation Study Bible* (Orlando: Ligonier Ministries / P & R Publishing Company, 2005), p. 379.

4. Oswald Chambers, *My Utmost for His Highest* (Grand Rapids, MI: Discovery House Publishers, 1992), October 17.

5. Matthew 6:19 (NASB).

6. Chambers, August 9.

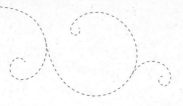

Other Harvest House Books
by Cindi McMenamin

God's Whispers to a Woman's Heart

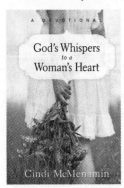

What is God whispering to *you*? Every moment of every day, He is at your side, ready to speak to your heart. He knows exactly how you feel and stands ready to respond—whether you are in need of wisdom, encouragement, or comfort. Let the heartwarming devotions in this book fill your days with the confident hope and peace that only God can give!

When a Mom Inspires Her Daughter

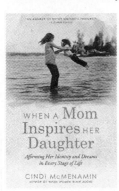

No matter what your daughter's age, God has given you a special and unique place from which to encourage, support, and inspire her. And there are many creative ways you can do that. Whether your girl is a child or an adult, or your relationship is strong or strained, this book offers a wealth of advice on ways you can enter your daughter's world and nurture a better relationship with her.

When Women Walk Alone

CINDI McMENAMIN

Every woman—whether she's single or married—has walked through the desert of loneliness. Whether you feel alone from being single, facing challenging life situations, or from being the spiritual head of your household, discover practical steps to finding support, transforming loneliness into spiritual growth, and turning your alone times into life-changing encounters with God.

Letting God Meet Your Emotional Needs

Do you long to have your emotional needs met, yet find that your husband or those close to you cannot always help bring fulfillment to your life? Discover true intimacy with God in this book that shows how to draw closer to the lover of your soul and find that He can, indeed, meet your deepest emotional needs.

When God Pursues a Woman's Heart

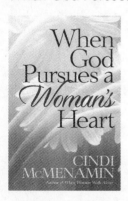

Within the heart of every woman is the desire to be cherished and loved. Recapture the romance of a relationship with God as you discover the many ways God loves you and pursues your heart as your hero, provider, comforter, friend, valiant knight, loving Daddy, perfect prince, and more.

When Women Long for Rest

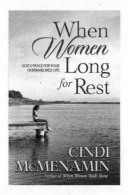

Women today are tired of feeling overwhelmed by all the demands on their lives and are longing for rest. They want to do more than just simplify or reorganize their lives. Here, Cindi invites women to find their quiet place at God's feet—a place where they can listen to Him, open their hearts to Him, and experience true rest.

When a Woman Discovers Her Dream

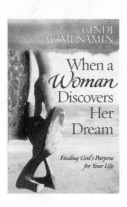

When it comes to living out the dream God has placed on your heart, do you shrug your shoulders and say, "It's too late for someone like me"? But you *can* live out that dream—no matter what your stage or place in life. Join Cindi as she shares how you can explore God's purposes for your life, make greater use of your special gifts, turn your dreams into reality, and become the masterpiece God designed you to be.

When a Woman Inspires Her Husband

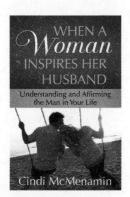

How can you become your husband's number one fan? God brought you alongside him to support him as only a wife can. Discover how you can be the encourager, motivator, inspiration, and admiration behind your husband—and the wind beneath his wings—as you understand his world, become his cheerleader, appreciate his differences, ease his burdens, and encourage him to dream.

When a Woman Overcomes Life's Hurts

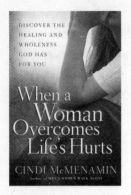

Only God can take the bitter things and turn them into blessings. But healing cannot take place until you replace the faulty thinking of our world with the truth about how God views you. You'll find this book filled with grace, redemption, and transformation that leads you toward a renewed focus on God and a resurgence of inner joy.

When You're Running on Empty

Do you feel as though you are running on empty? There is a way out. Cindi shares from her own life and struggles many helpful secrets about simplifying your priorities and obligations, rejuvenating yourself through God's Word, cultivating health habits that renew your energy, and learning to please God and not people.

Women on the Edge

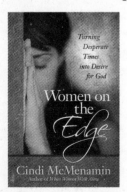

We all have times when we find ourselves dealing with stress that never seems to end. When that happens, we can either give up in resignation, or persevere and lean on the Lord. Rather than merely survive, choose to abundantly thrive—by learning how to yield all control of your life to God, and rest in His purpose and plan for your life.

When Couples Walk Together
(with Hugh McMenamin)

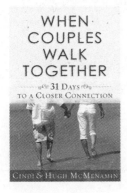

Are the demands of everyday life constantly pulling you and your spouse in different directions? If you've longed to rekindle the intimacy and companionship that first brought you together, join Hugh and Cindi as they share 31 days of simple, creative, and fun ways you can draw closer together again. You'll experience anew the joys of togetherness and unselfish love.

Parting Words of Encouragement

What legacy is God building into *your* life? Maybe
you're still wondering. I would love to hear from you
and encourage you, personally, and pray for you as well.

You can find me online at
www.StrengthForTheSoul.com

Leave me a message that you were there and let me know
how I can pray for you. I always respond to my readers.

You can also connect with me on Facebook at
Strength For The Soul

Or you can send me a letter at:
**Cindi McMenamin
c/o Harvest House Publishers
990 Owen Loop North
Eugene, OR 97402**

To contact me to speak for your group,
email me at **Cindi@StrengthForTheSoul.com**